1981

the
well-written
theme

Joan R. Walsky

1817

HARPER & ROW, PUBLISHERS, New York
Cambridge, Hagerstown, Philadelphia, San Francisco,
London, Mexico City, São Paulo, Sydney

For the people who taught me
and those who teach me now

Sponsoring Editor: Phillip Leininger
Project Editor: Eleanor Castellano
Designer: Robert Sugar
Production Manager: Marion A. Palen
Compositor: Tri-Star Graphics
Printer and Binder: The Murray Printing Company
Art Studio: Allyn-Mason Incorporated

The Well-Written Theme
Copyright © 1980 by Joan R. Walsky

Library of Congress Cataloging in Publication Data

Walsky, Joan R   Date-
  The Well-Written Theme.

  1. English language—Rhetoric.   I. Title.
PE1408.W31325   808'.042   79–20573
ISBN 0–06–046885–8

contents

iii

to the student

Writing well means learning to understand and work with a writing assignment efficiently and effectively so that you can express your ideas fully, clearly, and convincingly and proceed to something else. Thus, you have a twofold job. You will be learning about the "writing" part of it, about selecting and limiting a topic, about developing and expressing your ideas, and about polishing what you have said. But you will also be learning writing procedures that work, not only for college themes but for the kinds of writing you will be doing in the "real world" of politics, personal feelings, and job requirements.

This is one writing book that begins and remains with things as they are in the "real world." It works from a student's perspective, recognizing that learning to write well can be a time-consuming process at best, and that in the "real world" other pressures exist and, at times, other tasks will take priority over writing themes for freshman composition courses. With these realities in mind, this book focuses on what you need to know to do the job at hand. Abstractions and theory are left aside whenever possible, and instructions are clear and precise.

For the purposes of study, the book is divided into two units. In Unit One you will be learning about the rough draft. You will deal with the immediate problems of writing, with selecting and refining a topic, with gathering and evaluating ideas, and with structuring a theme and getting it on paper as acceptable paragraphs. These are the same skills you would apply in a "real world" writing situation, such as a job application or letter to the editor. The finer points of writing are left for the second unit.

This "first things first" approach takes you quickly and easily into the writing process. And along the way you will find information about how to solve some of the problems that students commonly face when writing themes. The glossary will be especially useful to you in this regard. If you take a few moments to look at it, you will find that it explains in checklist form what you need to know to move smoothly and efficiently through your theme-writing experience. You might want to pay special attention to the checklist of things to remember about writing college themes.

But most important of all, perhaps, is to have the confidence in yourself that you would need to master any new and challenging experience. If you will be patient with yourself and with what you are doing, you will find that you *can* write effectively and that you might even enjoy doing it.

Joan R. Walsky

unit One

the rough draft

chapter 1
getting started

1. The Writing Process

There are many entry points into the process of writing. Sometimes it starts with an idea you have, an opinion that needs to be expressed, a problem that you want to explore, or a solution that you want to share with other people. These are the ideal beginnings because you are already committed to them before you start to write. Your interest and enthusiasm as you discover new ideas and arguments and the best and most convincing ways of expressing them will help carry you through the writing process. And your own enthusiasm will help excite and involve your reader in what you have said.

The most fundamental reason, in fact, for studying "writing" at all is to develop your ability to explain your own ideas clearly to other people and to convince them that the issues to which you yourself are committed are valid or, at the very least, worth considering. Whether you want to write a letter to the editor or work for a political candidate, you will use the same writing techniques that you develop in your composition classes. And no matter what you plan to do for a living, you will probably have to apply your writing skills at one time or another. At some point on most job ladders these days, a promotion will hinge on the candidate's ability to express ideas clearly and cogently, aloud and in writing. In this sense, too, your writing classes will be well worth the effort that they will require of you.

What do you do and how do you start?

Let us suppose, to begin with, that you have a "real-life" situation that seems to require a written response from you. It could be anything—a job application, a letter complaining about the maintenance in your apartment complex, or a note requesting information about a product or company. But for the purposes of this example let us assume that you must use the public-transportation system in your city and that the system has recently been changed for the worse. Calling the company has done no good, since the phone operators have no control over the system. So you have decided to write a letter of protest with a copy to the editor of your city's newspaper. In this case you already know why you are going to write (you are angry, wish to complain, and want to see changes made), to whom (the bus company), when (when the mood suits), and about what (changes in the bus system). Your next step, probably, would be to sit down with a pen and paper to note ideas and specifics: Exactly what is bothering you and exactly what do you want done about it? You are in effect clarifying your issue. You would do this automatically in your own mind, even if you did not bother to record it on paper. But we will record it this time.

General Issue: Decline of Bus Service

1. Before change, bus service was adequate if not good. Had to wait about ten minutes to catch the first bus to school in the morning, and then about five minutes to transfer. The same to go to work in the afternoon. Then just one bus home.
2. Since the change, the service has been lousy.
3. In the morning, the first bus arrives seven minutes *after* the second one leaves, meaning that I must wait thirty minutes. The same is true in the afternoon. Evening bus ride has not been affected.
4. Wait for transfer buses alone now amounts to one hour per day.
5. I am furious.

You can see how an effective letter—or an effective theme—might develop out of just such a simple list of ideas. You might begin by adding some details and some connecting words so that your reader could follow the discussion easily. And of course you would make complete sentences out of the bits and pieces.

Bus Service—Draft 1

1. Before the change in bus routes that took place three weeks ago, bus service was adequate if not good. I had to wait about ten minutes to catch the first bus to school in the morning, and then about five minutes to pick up my transfer bus. I followed the same procedure to get to my part-time job in the afternoon, while going home required that I catch a single bus.
2. Since the change in routing, however, bus service has been lousy.
3. In the morning my first bus arrives seven minutes *after* the bus I must transfer to leaves. That means I must wait thirty minutes for the next bus. The same is true when I try to get to work in the afternoon. My evening bus ride has not be affected.
4. With a little simple arithmetic, you can see that your "improved" bus schedules have cost me an additional hour's wait each day for the buses I must take to get where I must go. I want you to know that I am absolutely furious about this matter.

If this were your letter, you would ask yourself a few questions about it before recopying it to send out.

Does it get your message across to your intended reader? Is the problem clear? Would your reader be able to take the actions you wanted from the information you provided? Could you express yourself more adequately?

Whether or not you would decide to revise the letter before sending it out would depend on several things, including how important the issue was to you and how much time you had to spend on the letter. With the letter as it is, your reader would not know precisely what your problem was. For example, what buses must you take, when and where? What kind of response do you expect? Are you asking for a letter of apology or do you want scheduling changes to improve your situation or are you requesting a return to the old schedules? A few moments' thought would help you clarify your expectations in your letter and thus help your reader provide you with the service you want.

Specific Issue: The Decline in Service Since the Change in Schedules and Routes Went into Effect Three Weeks Ago

1. Since the change in schedules and routes went into effect three weeks ago, bus service in my area has seriously declined—to the point where many people are investigating alternate forms of transportation.

2. It is not clear why the changes were made or what purpose they were intended to serve.
3. However, the changes have made service lousy. Now all interconnecting buses that run from the Maplewood tract to downtown miss each other by about seven minutes.
4. In my case, I must take the 23B to Rosewood and Maple at 7 A.M. and pick up the 18 to go downtown. As you will discover if you check your copy of your schedule, the connections are such that I must wait about thirty minutes for the 18.
5. I have the same problem in the afternoon, when the 18 misses the 9Y, and again I must wait thirty minutes.
6. I am seriously considering buying a car, which I can't afford, and will have to do so unless you can provide more workable schedules.

A letter that you developed from this list of specific facts would tell your reader at the bus company exactly what was bothering you. It would begin by identifying the cause of the problem (changes in routes) and the time factor (three weeks ago) *and* by highlighting the importance of the problem to the bus company (people will drive to work). It is a truism that people are always more interested in problems that affect them than in other kinds of problems, and thus will pay more attention to the former. Pinpointing the relationship between your writing topic (decline in service) and your reader (bus company personnel) helps make your ideas relevant and in that way maximizes their impact. And paragraphs three through five give the person at the bus company enough specific information (which buses are involved, at what times) to make useful suggestions without having to write an interim letter to you requesting more information.

In this, as in many parts of your theme-writing process, you are applying ideas and data and skills that *you already have*. If this were *your* letter and *your* problem, you would already know all the details that appear in the second version of the letter, though you might not bother to write out the list. In your own mind you would already know your purpose for writing: You would already know whether you were simply writing to vent your anger or whether you wanted specific actions to be taken in your behalf, and if so, what actions.

Thus, as you compose any letter (or theme), you must remember to consider your reader. What questions will your reader have about your topic? What information about your situation will be needed before your reader can act in your behalf? The first person to read your letter may not be the person you want to talk to (for example, a corporate vice president is unlikely to be the first person to read your letter even if it is addressed to him or her), and your reader, in any case, may not be inclined to act in your behalf.

Your job as a writer is to provide the information your reader needs to understand your message in a clear and usable fashion so that your communication may be completed successfully and your reader will, at the very least, know what you want. Listing your ideas before you write will help you to evaluate the positions you are taking, to include enough specific data so that your reader will understand, and to move easily into the writing process because you've already gathered the "something to say."

Consider the following issue lists to see if you as the reader would understand what was troubling the writer and would be able to respond appropriately.

A

Issue: Phone Company, High Bills

1. In the past year and a half, my phone bill has increased tremendously. I do not understand the reason for this.
2. When I first moved into my apartment, I was paying about half of what you are now charging. It makes me very angry to get my bill each month and see the increase.
3. With the cost of living going up for everybody, and with many people on fixed incomes and unable to pay more, it is a crime for you to raise your rates. I am going to complain to my congressman if I get another high bill like the last one.
4. Please do something about this situation immediately.

If you were the person at the phone company who had to read and respond to a letter that contained these ideas, what would you do? It is clear that the writer is angry and wants some kind of response. Do you know enough to determine why the phone bill has increased so dramatically?

Plainly, you do not. Before acting, you would need to know how much the writer was and is paying, what calls are being made and at what times of day, and whether or not any new charges are involved (did the person get a second phone, for example?). You might be able to look this information up in your records, and would probably do so.

But you could have answered this letter much more quickly and easily if it had provided the information in the first place.

B

Specific Issue: 50 Percent Increase in My Phone Bill Within 18 Months Without Increase in Service

1. In the past year and a half, my phone bill has increased by 50 percent (from an average of $30 per month to an average of $45 per month), without any change or improvement in my phone service. I make no more toll calls than previously, and still have just the one phone.
2. I do not understand the reason for this tremendous jump, and I am quite angry about it.
3. If I do not receive a reasonable explanation from you within three weeks (by June 30), I will send copies of this letter and my bill history to the commission that regulates you and ask it to investigate.

The second approach gives the customer service representative specific facts about the phone bill that could be verified or refuted by a check of the records. Perhaps the customer has indeed been making more long-distance calls. Perhaps not. But in either case the second approach sticks to the point that is most important to the writer, helps the reader understand that point by providing specific data, and helps the reader respond appropriately by clarifying what is wanted and the importance of the response.

C

Issue: Dangerous Intersection in My Neighborhood

1. One particular intersection in my neighborhood is extremely dangerous and has been the scene of several accidents over the past few months.
2. It is a very busy street in a residential neighborhood.
3. It is on the pathway to the local school, and many children must cross each day.
4. There is no stoplight at any corner.
5. There are four-way stop signs, some of which are obscured by high shrubs.
6. Some friends and I think that something must be done about this situation before someone is killed.

What is your evaluation of this list of facts? Would you understand the situation? You probably would, up to a point. Yet you would not know which intersection was involved and precisely what the writer wanted to see done about it. Although the importance of the situation has been made clear, you still might not know how to respond.

D

Specific Issue: Need to Install Stoplights at the Intersection of Madison and Vine

1. With the increase in the traffic flow down Madison Street since the Consolidated plant went into operation six months ago, the intersection of Madison and Vine has become an extremely dangerous place, especially for the children who must cross to attend Butler Elementary School.
2. Madison and Vine had always been a quiet, residential area, with beautiful homes and tall shrubs and many trees. A stop sign on each corner had been enough to handle the traffic—before the plant.
3. Now, however, the shrubs and trees are a menace because they obscure the stop signs and make it difficult to see children in a crosswalk when you are making a right turn.
4. Within the past three months, three children have been struck by cars. Fortunately, none of the injuries has been serious, and all of the children have recovered.
5. But we need to get stoplights on those corners and have the shrubs trimmed or removed before someone is killed. We must take action immediately.

Because it is more specific and thus more clear, the second letter will have a far greater impact on a reader. The reader can say, "I understand and I agree; what can I do to help?" In a real situation, since this letter would be sent to somebody with predictable authority (such as a newspaper editor or a person on the city council), the writer would be in a position to specify further what should be done (if you agree with me, write to the city council; if you do not take action immediately, I will begin a recall petition; if you want to discuss this matter with me, I can be reached at this phone number during working hours). The point is that, as the writer, you would *already* have all the particulars at your command. Providing them to your reader is a simple step, but one that is vital to the communication process.

EXERCISE 1
Consider the following general "issue" situations in terms of what you learned in the preceding section. Will the reader understand the situation fully? Write a "specific-issue" list for each situation, inventing those details which would be needed to clarify the issue and the desired response. Prepare your lists before reading on to the commentary.

A

Issue: Getting a Job

1. I am interested in getting a job with your company.
2. I am a good worker and very reliable. I take directions very well and am hardly ever absent.
3. A lot of people have been pleased with my work, and I am able to send you many references.
4. I hope to hear from you very soon.

B

Issue: Broken Toy

1. This Christmas I bought one of your toys for my niece.
2. The toy was heavily advertised on television, and all the children in the neighborhood wanted it.
3. However, I am very dissatisfied with the performance of the toy.
4. Within a few moments after she had unwrapped it, she had cut herself on an exposed screw.
5. Within several hours, I had to make repairs to major components.
6. A few days later, the toy was junk.
7. I think I am entitled to a refund.

C

Issue: Job Opportunities with the Clay Company

1. I have received your letter requesting information about job opportunities with the Clay Company.
2. As you know, we make many products and employ many people at our several locations.
3. Given our operation, we require people with many kind of skills, and hire them according to our needs and the job market.
4. If I can be of any further help, please do not hesitate to write to me.

In each instance the issue has not been made clear to the reader. In issue A, it is not clear what kind of job the writer is applying for and what qualifications and other assets he or she has. What kind of toy are we talking about in issue B? What does the Clay Company do? How many plants or offices are in operation, and what opportunities are available right now? Read these revised lists and compare them with your own. How do the details help?

D

Specific Issue: Getting a Part-Time Office Job at Hartford & Western

1. I would like very much to speak with you about a part-time job in your law office.
2. I intend to make law my career, and want to get as much exposure to the profession as possible while I am still in school.
3. I am a freshman student studying business administration. I have good office skills (I type 55 words per minute), am reliable, and want very much to learn.
4. I have included several letters of recommendation along with my resume.
5. I will call you in a week or so to set up an appointment at your convenience.

E

Specific Issue: Redford Cooking Oven—A Dangerous, Defective Toy

1. This Christmas I bought one of your Redford cooking ovens for my 9-year-old niece, who is about the same age as the children playing with the toy in your television ads.
2. Within a few moments after she had unwrapped it, she had cut herself on an exposed screw at the bottom of the oven, and a few moments later the door came off and had to be repaired.
3. The performance of the toy went downhill from there, and it was scrapped within a week.
4. I think I am entitled to an immediate refund for the entire purchase price of this dangerous, defective toy. And I think further that you should take if off the market or have it substantially redesigned before someone really gets hurt or sues you.

F

**Specific Issue: Jobs Now Available at the Clay
Company**

1. I have received your letter requesting information about job opportunities with the Clay Company.
2. Clay manufactures containers for novelty items for its own and other product lines, and serves as a warehouse and distribution center for many of its clients' products.
3. At the moment we have several positions open on our assembly line; we also have one job open in our warehouse and two secretarial jobs available in our main office. I have attached job descriptions for your use. In addition, we have several openings for our summer intern program, which might also interest you.
4. If you think you qualify for any of these positions, and are interested in applying, please send me your resume or drop by and we can talk. You will need to act quickly, since we will be filling these positions within the next two weeks.

You can see how the addition of specifics helps clarify an issue for a reader (and focus it for the writer as well). In most cases you as a writer will have the details you need in your possession or know where to find them. Your main challenge will be in remembering to include the details in the rush of things you must consider, and in determining exactly which details will be appropriate for the reader you wish to reach.

EXERCISE 2
Think of a situation in your own life that has been bothering you or of an issue about which you are concerned. Write an "issue" list of ideas for preparing a letter on the subject. Deliberately leave out details that you know would be useful for your reader in order to keep your list general. Then prepare a second, "specific-issue" list of ideas, including the details you think your reader will need to have to fully understand your point of view.

Examine your two lists and the thought processes that you went through to create them. Specifically, how are the lists different? What did you do differently in the two cases? Your goal is to recognize the differences in the lists and in your own thought processes so that you may apply what you have learned here to the theme-writing process. If you can recognize and make a "specific list," you have taken a big step toward being able to write successfully.

2. Your First College Writing Assignments

Ideally, as we saw earlier, the impetus for any writing project comes from you. You are angry about something, or pleased, or curious, and you decide what to write and when and to whom and at what point to stop revising and send the thing on its way. But more often, and more realistically in terms of your college experience, the impetus for a writing project will come from outside—from a professor—in the form of an assignment of one sort or another. When this happens, it is important for you to have a firm idea of how to proceed so that you can get started with as little hesitation as possible and complete the assignment successfully in a reasonable amount of time.

Many students are surprised by the writing process—by the fact that they usually cannot sit down, select a topic, and simply write. You may be surprised if it happens to you. But if it happens to you, you are perfectly normal.

You might expect to "sit down and write" a theme because that is what *seems* to happen when you initiate the writing project yourself. You are angry about the change in the bus schedules; you decide to write; you sit down and write.

In fact, though, you took a number of prewriting steps before you ever put a word on paper, and you make and, as you write, continue to make many interrelated decisions about your subject and your purpose and your audience—whether you are aware of these processes or not.

What would you have done naturally if you yourself had written that letter to the bus company?

Even if you never put a word on paper as you did it, you would decide on your reason for writing (you were angry), on your audience (a bus company official), and on your topic (the decline in service since the new schedules went into effect). And you must take *the same steps* when you write your themes. It will help you focus your efforts if you put your thoughts on paper.

What is the reason for your theme-writing assignment? Sometimes a theme is assigned to allow you to practice a certain skill, such as limiting a topic or organizing ideas. In these cases you will want to pay special attention to the specified writing aspect. Other times a theme is assigned to test your understanding of a concept or a reading assignment. This will frequently occur in history and philosophy classes and in other "non-English" writing classes. And at certain times it will occur in your composition classes as well. In many cases students will decide that they "can't write" or that writing is difficult when the actual problem is that they haven't understood the reading assignment or the concept to be practiced is not clear. Writing itself will demand your best skill and ability. If you need to understand the assignment or ask questions about the concept, you should take care of these preliminaries before you sit down to write.

Good writing also takes time and concentration. It takes time for you to develop and express your ideas, to search for the details you need to make your concepts clear, and to revise in order to maximize the impact of what you are saying. It is not fair to yourself to expect, as many students do, to sit down and complete a theme in twenty minutes. And it is not fair to yourself to leave the whole writing job for the last minute. Such a procedure compresses your writing into an unnatural and stressful process: You must produce the right ideas in the right order and right now. No wonder writing seems unpleasant.

When writing works naturally, you will be taking a certain amount of your time to think and understand and reason and to get used to the topic, if one is assigned, or to select one, if that is appropriate. If you have a week to do the work, it would not be unreasonable to use the first two days to plan and question and jot down ideas. You would not have to devote a large amount of time to the process so long as you were genuinely proceeding with it.

The planning allows you to uncover any questions or problems that should be dealt with and to deal with them by doing any necessary background reading or asking appropriate questions before writing your paragraphs.

On the third or fourth day, you should plan to set aside some quiet time, free from distractions, and preferably during the part of the day when you normally are at your best. During this hour or two, you will perform "rough-draft" procedures. You will limit (or select and limit) your topic, analyze your audience, formulate your thesis sentence (a statement of the main idea for your paper), gather and evaluate ideas, organize your ideas, and write the paragraphs that make up an initial draft. You will learn more about each of these procedures as you progress through the chapters of this unit.

Then, depending on the importance of the theme, you will set aside a certain amount of time to work further on your rough draft. You will check to make sure that your ideas do support your thesis sentence, that the ideas are in a sensible order, and that you have not omitted anything of importance. All of this occurs before you begin on the process that we are calling revision.

Revision, the subject of the second unit of this book, focuses on the elegance of what you are saying, the completeness of your paragraphs, the variety of overall and paragraph structures and the blend of sentence types and rhythms, and on the very words that you select to express your ideas. Concentrating on these finer points can be in your way when you are attempting to build an acceptable rough draft, which is the reason for postponing them as you are learning to write.

But even rough drafts should be written *more than once.*

It is unlikely that you will find the best way of saying what you want to say on your first attempt; few people can. So you need to be willing to try again, even to the point of discarding a first rough draft and starting over. Each time you write, each time you attempt to express your ideas clearly and forcefully, you will be learning more and more about the kinds of choices writers must make. Each time you write, you will grow in experience and ability. An important part of learning to write effectively on any subject is being willing to experiment with what you have to say in order to discover the "best" way of expressing your ideas.

And you will find that the very same "specific-issue" list can lead to many different themes or letters. Here, for example, are three letters that students developed from the specific-issue list earlier in this chapter.

A

Dear Mr. Jones:

This letter is to inform you that the quality of your service has declined seriously since the new scheduling went into effect on April 21. As a daily user of bus lines, I wish to register my strongest protest.

Since the new scheduling went into effect, all interconnecting buses miss each other by about seven minutes. In other words, if you must take a 23B to Rosewood and Maple to pick up an 18 to go downtown, the 18 will have left seven minutes before the 23B is scheduled to arrive. This means that you have to wait a half-hour before the next 18 arrives.

Since I must make this sort of connection twice during each working day (I have to catch an 18 and connect with the 9Y each afternoon), I lose one hour—count them, *60* minutes—each day because of the incompetence of your scheduling process.

Please rethink this scheduling process immediately and make changes as appropriate to improve service (return to the old schedules or devise new ones that work properly) before all your riders decide to buy cars or to hitchhike.

Sincerely yours,

B

Dear Mr. Jones:

Since your change in scheduling which occurred on April 21, it has taken me an extra hour each day to get from where I live to school and from school to my job. This is because the 23B arrives at Rosewood and Maple 7 minutes after the 18 leaves for downtown, and the 18 arrives after the 9Y departs. It seems to me that you could schedule your buses more effectively.

Please let me know what can be done to improve this situation.

Sincerely yours,

C

Dear Mr. Jones:

Since your new schedules went into effect three weeks ago, bus service in this city has gone to hell.

People are waiting longer—much longer—to catch the same decrepit old buses which have air conditioning only on winter days and working heaters only in the summer sun. Fares went up for many people, all of those who must transfer from buses to the subways, which themselves are only marginally acceptable. And bus schedules seem to have been worked out by a drunken monkey hopping about on hot coals for dear life. The point of scheduling, as it seems to me, is to facilitate the transportation process—which means that buses which should interconnect do in fact interconnect.

I am unfortunate enough to have to use the buses to get to school and to work. I must get a 23B to the corner of Rosewood and Maple to pick up an 18 to get downtown. Since you have "improved" the schedules, the 18 leaves seven minutes *before* the 23B arrives. Similarly, in the afternoon, the 18 arrives several minutes after the 9Y is scheduled to depart. Surely you can do better.

You have your city at the point of armed rebellion. People who own cars and had previously left them home are starting to drive (which does not help the traffic any). Fewer riders mean that you will probably have to raise fares again to support your current level of incompetence which will lead to fewer riders. And paying more is always good consolation for worse service.

People, like myself, who don't own cars are looking to purchase them. And in the meantime the thumbs and fingers in this city are being exercised as never before: the thumbs to catch rides, and the certain fingers to indicate an opinion of bus company officials.

If you think you can straighten this mess out, you had better get started before you are replaced. I figure you have about two months to get the job done.

Sincerely yours,

Even though these three letters are "about" the same topic, they are very different in style and in tone, or the attitude the writer takes toward the subject and the reader. The first letter is informative, if a bit angry ("I wish to register my protest"; "I lose one hour—count them, *60 minutes*—because of the incompetence of your scheduling process"). The writer states the point firmly and in some detail. The second letter is both shorter and milder than the first. It explains the situation without wasting words, expresses some disappointment ("It seems to me that you could schedule your buses more effectively"), and requests information and help.

The third letter starts out with an attention-getting, aggressive opening sentence ("Bus service in this city has gone to hell"), and proceeds to a detailed attack on several elements of the bus system. This letter, the longest, covers ideas that are not present in the others, and states all those ideas very strongly ("You have your city at the point of armed rebellion") and at times in less than elegant language.

There is clearly more than one acceptable way to express any idea. Your job as a writer is to consider the alternatives available to you. Will you be firm and formal? Will you be angry? Will you strive for a reasoned protest, or is your goal to use telling examples to make your point strike home? What you decide now will help shape the scope and quality of your theme as a whole.

EXERCISE 1

Evaluate the following specific-issue list which a student developed in preparation for filling out a job application. Would this be an adequate list for a 400- to 700-word discussion? If not, rewrite the list, inventing details as necessary; then use the list as the basis for writing a three-paragraph discussion. Your goal is to explain your ideas clearly and completely to your reader. Don't worry about "fancy" language or sentence structure, although your work should be grammatically correct.

Specific-Issue List—Application for Employment

1. I have education relevant to the job.
2. I get pretty good grades in school.
3. I haven't had much experience in working in general, but I try hard.
4. I think I would be good working in your store because I get along well with all kinds of people.
5. I promise to do my very best on the job.

EXERCISE 2

Determining what facts and other information your reader will need to understand your ideas and presenting those facts effectively are among the most critical writing skills. If your reader cannot understand what you have to say, you have failed as a communicator. Since your reader will not be able to ask questions of you, you must be especially careful to be precise and complete in your written presentations.

For the purpose of practicing these skills, you are about to undertake an exercise that requires the cooperation of your classmates or another audience who can respond to your written directions. The exercise has two parts.

You begin by drawing a geometric figure in the center of a piece of paper. Use circles, squares, triangles, and other figures to create a pattern that pleases you, but don't make it too complicated. Figure 1 will give you some idea of what you might draw.

Now take a separate piece of paper and *list the steps* that a reader would have to take to recreate the figure you have invented—with the following audience analysis in mind.

Your reader knows how to use a pen or pencil, is basically literate, and can draw a straight or curved line. However, this reader never learned the names of geometric figures. In other words, you cannot give instructions such as "Draw a triangle" because your reader will not understand what you mean. You must explain how to put the straight and curved lines together to produce the figure.

Using labels ("point A"), precise details ("a horizontal line three inches long"), and an appropriate presentation order ("begin by . . . then do . . .") will help your reader understand and follow your instructions.

SAMPLE FIGURES

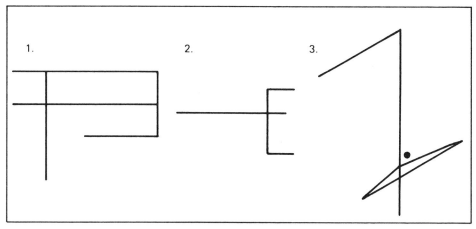

Figure 1

Exchange instruction lists (but not geometric designs) with a classmate. Have that person follow your instructions. Then evaluate the results: Does the figure look like the one you had in mind (and on paper)? Where did your instructions break down? What details were missing? Discuss your experience with your partner so that both of you understand where the communication process succeeded and where it did not.

As an alternative, you may read your instructions to several classmates, who will draw on the blackboard in response. It is best if you don't look while they draw (if you watch, you will be tempted to correct what they are doing). When you turn around you will probably see that you have more than one response to your instructions and that at least a few of the chalk illustrations don't much resemble your pen-and-ink drawing.

As you analyze the results of your experiment, you will need to consider the fact that you as a communicator cannot control what your reader (or listener) will do with your information. Each person has different expectations and a different world view, and each person responds differently to the same set of words. Some people pay attention and follow instructions; others do not.

As a communicator, it is your job to convey your messages as clearly and precisely and interestingly as you can to maximize the likelihood that your ideas will be transmitted to your reader or listener. While you cannot control what happens to your communication after it leaves you, you can control it before it reaches your audience. Experiments such as this one will help give you the kind of feedback you need to evaluate your work and improve its quality and precision.

EXERCISE 3

It is important that you be able to distinguish between what will probably be your first attempts to get any theme on paper and what we are calling an "acceptable rough draft," or the first copy your instructor will normally see.

Most writers spend some time, once they have specific-issue lists, working to form complete sentences and paragraphs that express their ideas. Sometimes the ideas seem to flow smoothly; other times drafts must be started and stopped and started again. Each attempt will not necessarily result in a rough draft—something many beginning writers don't know.

An acceptable rough draft sticks to a single topic; all interesting but irrelevant material has been eliminated. It explains a single main idea about that topic; this is called the "thesis sentence" idea. If, for example, your main idea is that "children should not be allowed to watch television," all of your points explain and clarify and defend that idea. Each of your main defending points, too, is explained and exemplified in a paragraph or so. Your goal is to have your reader understand your discussion because you have explained yourself clearly and in enough detail without wasting words on trivia.

As you read the following student themes, notice that the first one is not an acceptable rough draft because it is incomplete and wanders away from the topic. The second uses a simple but effective support structure to explain the student's point of view.

Analyze the third theme. Would it, in your judgment, be an acceptable rough draft? Why? Be prepared to defend your conclusions in class.

A

Children and Television

Children should not be allowed to watch television. That's what I believe. What is more, I have always believed that.

When I was a child there was no television in my house because my parents did not believe in it. In fact, we had plenty of money and my parents could have had a television set, one in every room in fact, but they didn't do it because they didn't believe in it.

I too don't believe that children should be allowed to watch television. Don't you?

B

Children and Television

Children should not be allowed to watch television. There are many reasons why this is true, but I will focus on what I believe to be the most important of them.

First, while there are many things that children can learn from television, their time could be better spent in other ways such as interacting with other people (children and adults, including their parents), looking at books and magazines, running and jumping, and even doing nothing, for doing nothing is a part of growing up too.

Second, television teaches children things that it might be better for all of us if they didn't learn. For example, violence is a way of life (which may be true). Violence also doesn't hurt anyone, as cartoon characters reassemble themselves after disasters occur. After years of television, violence is simply acceptable or ignored.

Finally, *watching* television teaches children that life is about *watching* rather than *doing.* Nothing could be further from the truth in today's society. While you can learn a bit about tennis from watching tennis matches on television, that does not exercise your heart or lungs or muscles, nor does it build your competitive spirit. You don't learn how to get along with people from watching television. You don't learn how to plan a course and follow it in spite of obstacles. And you don't learn how to earn money or spend it wisely. All you learn from watching television is how to watch television, and we are a nation of experts at that.

C

Children and Television

I can't quite decide whether I think that children should be allowed to watch television or not, but on balance, it would probably be better for small ones if they didn't watch at all or if their viewing was limited to no more than an hour or at the most two hours per day.

Children *do* learn things from television, important things like vocabulary and language skills. And children's TV has programs that teach young ones about mathematics and science and getting along with other people. For many children television time would otherwise be empty time, devoid of parental attention or anything worth doing.

Yet it is too easy for a busy parent to plant the child in front of the television set and go about a day's work. And it is also true that children learn bad habits from television: to be a spectator instead of a participant, that killing is a way of life, that pain can be inflicted, as it is on cartoon characters, without hurting and without permanent damage. All in all, if parents would not rely on television, children might turn back to books, from which they could also learn vocabulary and language skills as well as mathematics and science, or to each other and the family, from whom they could best learn to get along with other people.

EXERCISE 4

Think of a topic in your daily life that interests you. It should be something you know about, like a problem in your neighborhood or home, but something that is not too complex, like a problem in international relations. If possible, it should be something that you think would be of interest to others. You might, for example, pick the problem of getting reliable newspaper delivery or sharing a bathroom with several people—something that most people can relate to.

Once you have a topic, prepare a specific-issue list like those that dealt with the phone bill and stoplight problems. You may want to include humorous items on your list, if you can think of any, since they will help make your theme come to life for your reader.

When you have a specific-issue list in hand, write what you consider to be an acceptable rough draft, remembering to stick to a single topic, explain a single main idea, explain each of your main supporting ideas in a paragraph or so, and eliminate all irrelevant material. Plan on three to five paragraphs.

Revise your rough draft according to your instructor's comments.

chapter 2

the preliminary stages

1. Specifying Your Topic

It is a fact that, as a beginning writer, the first thing you will be faced with when you are assigned a theme to write is the topic. Whether you select a topic yourself or one is assigned to you, knowing how to handle your topic properly is clearly your first priority.

Most often, in your college writing classes, you will be assigned either a topic, a choice of topics, or an overall topic area (for example, "Write a theme about happiness") that you will have to restrict and define. We will deal with the special problems of the unfamiliar or uncongenial topic in the next chapter. For now, however, let us focus on the times when you have a free choice of topics. In that way you can learn how topics should be handled in general before you must cope with an especially difficult one.

If you are selecting your own topic, you will want to choose one that (1) is worthy of your time and attention, (2) requires no expertise that you cannot acquire quickly (you don't want to burden yourself unnecessarily with a complex research assignment), and (3) is small enough in scope so that you can discuss its ideas fully in the number of words you plan to write and the amount of time at your disposal.

A topic like "happiness" or "philosophy" or "wars" or "politics" would be far too large to cover effectively. If you try, several things are likely to happen, as they did in the following student themes.

A

Happiness

Happiness is one of the most important things in life. It means many things to many people. All over the world, people define happiness differently. What makes you happy may not make me happy and vice versa.

In a search for happiness, nothing is too much to do. Sometimes I think it is money that makes you happy. Other times I think it is peace of mind. Still other times, I think it must be long life.

B

Fun

Splashing in the surf is one of the ways I like to spend my spare time having fun. You should know, however, that believe it or not I also enjoy class. Learning to write can be fun if you have the right attitude.

Several years ago, I took a class that wasn't so much fun even though my attitude was excellent. The teacher was very boring, mean, and unfair to the students whose work she was supposed to evaluate. No wonder her class was not fun. But overall, school has been a pleasant experience for me and one which I would recommend to people of all ages.

C

Careers

There are many career possibilities open to college students these days. You could be a doctor or lawyer, teacher or engineer. You could also undertake to learn trades such as being a fireman or plumber since college does not always have to be relevant to what you finally do in life.

Most students begin planning for their careers when they are in junior high. They investigate possibilities and learn about job requirements. Then they gear their minds and their studies to their chosen fields of endeavor.

Because the topics for these students' compositions were large and general, the themes themselves rambled along, staying on the surface of the experience, spending words without saying much of anything. It seems as if the students did not know where to get started or what to say.

If the students had selected smaller and more specific topics, it would have been much easier for them to handle the writing process and the resulting themes would have been far more satisfying. In fact, that is what occurred when the students revised the themes, selecting as topics subcategories of their original ideas.

D

One Happy Moment in My Life

In my life, which has been full of happy moments, one stands out as different from all the rest, as in every way more special, more profound.

Usually, in stories like this, the narrator begins by telling what an ordinary day it was when the event occurred. But that is not true in this case. This day was not ordinary, for this day held the birth of my first child, a little girl, a beautiful and precious Amy Beth Walker.

The moment I am talking about is that instant in which I saw and held her for the very first time. Nothing like that experience had ever happened to me before, and nothing remotely as glorious has happened to me since. For all my life, I will remember that moment and be grateful for it.

E

Having Fun—Cheap

If you've ever been a student, you know the importance that having fun can have in your life. Just maintaining your sanity requires a certain amount of time devoted solely to the pursuit of pleasure. But if you've been a student, you probably also know that money can be hard to come by, and that having fun "cheap" is an important skill to develop.

Before I read the book on mind control, I had tried all the normal ways of having fun: movies, beach, trips to the mountains, shows, surfing, women, booze, going home for vacation, not going home for vacation. And they were fun. But they cost money, some more than others, but all required the long green.

The book on mind control (available for $1.95 or I'll loan you my copy) showed me how to enjoy each moment, to focus my attention on the here and now, to center myself in what I was doing rather than wishing I was doing something (anything) else. Even though I'm not perfect at it yet, I have found that such concentration on the present and acceptance of it has made every activity more fun, again, some more than others, and that this change in outlook can be accomplished by any student—cheap.

F

The Closing of a Career Path

It may sound dumb to you, but all my life I have wanted to be a teacher, and to teach young children. Maybe first through third grades.

It seems to me that such a career means that I could have an important impact on the lives of many people. Children who have good experiences in their early grades in school tend to enjoy school more and to do better through their education. However, I have found that being a grade school teacher is not a good way to earn a living.

Unfortunately, there are too many teachers on the market and too few jobs. I have not yet determined how I will cope with this frustration of my lifelong career goal—whether I will study to be a teacher and hope for the best, or whether I will select a second alternative. But it seems a shame to me that a career path could be closed to a generation of American students in this fashion and that persons like myself will not have a chance to contribute to society where they most want to do so.

The revised themes are superior to the originals *because they go more deeply into a smaller topic.* Each writer conveys a sense of personal interest in the story being told. The details are there to bring the theme to life for the reader, and each theme provides a satisfying sense of completeness—of a topic treated fully.

As you are selecting your theme topics, you will want to pick areas that are important to you (you may not be able to control this aspect when topics are assigned, of course). It is probably OK to write a 500-word theme about your dinner last night *if* that dinner had some special meaning in your life. If it was just an ordinary dinner, why bother? And while it may be tempting to try to write a theme about a new philosophy you are studying or the scientific discovery you read about in the newspaper, you may find that second thoughts are in order. Before you spend too much time on such a topic, you will have to ensure that you can get enough information about it so that you can discuss it fully, and that you can understand the information you get (that is, that the information will not be too technical) quickly enough so that you have time to work it into an effective theme.

It may help you understand the concept of a specific topic if you consider the thought processes that went into the letter of complaint to the bus company. You had a general area of complaint (you were mad at the bus company), which is akin to a *general topic area.* But you also had a specific area of complaint, which is like the *specific topic* you are looking for to make your writing job easier. The more specific you can be, the easier your writing job will become. So you analyze the general complaint area to determine what your specific complaint might be.

You are not just mad at the bus company. You are angry because the scheduling was fouled up. More specifically, you are angry because the interconnecting buses you depend on each day have been rescheduled so that you have to wait an extra thirty minutes at two different times each day.

General Topic Area ⟶ *More Specific Topic* ⟶ *More Specific Topic*

Angry at bus ⟶ Schedules fouled ⟶ 23B to Rosewood and
company.   up.   Maple misses 18 to
                                                                          downtown by 30
                                                                          minutes at 7 A.M.; 18
                                                                          misses 9Y in afternoon
                                                                          by same amount of
                                                                          time.

As you focus more closely on your specific topic, you eliminate ideas that are irrelevant or tangentially relevant, which means that you know what you will *not* have to discuss to make your point clear. You will not, for example, have to discuss the history of bus transportation in your city (except insofar as it relates to your specific topic). You will not waste your own time or your reader's with nonessential material. And at the same time it becomes easier to select the kinds of essential details your reader must have to really understand what you mean.

Similarly, if you are asked to write about an experience in your life, you will need to focus your attention on a specific experience, or part of one, so that you can provide the kinds of rich detail that will bring the experience to life for your reader. It is not possible to cover a large amount of territory in a few words without being superficial and unconvincing.

If you set out to write a theme about "college," you would be overwhelmed by the number of possibilities and places to start and paths to follow in your discussion. Similarly, you could not discuss "the Red Cross" or "your hobbies" in 250 or 500 or even 1000 words. You would need to make a more specific selection within the topic itself.

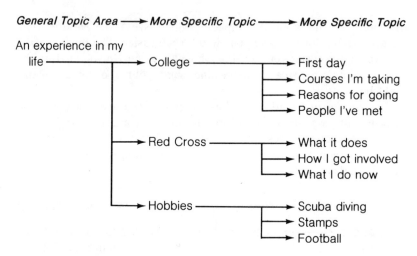

General Topic Area ⟶ *More Specific Topic* ⟶ *More Specific Topic*

You are looking for some specific subcategory of the general topic area, an event or instance or idea or something that has had an impact on you, has been important to you, and seems worth explaining to someone else. You are looking for a topic that you can handle right now, preferably relying on research to get supporting details if necessary but not for basic information, and one that can be treated fully in the number of words you plan to write.

Starting with a topic that is too big or vague or difficult and research oriented or meaningless is the fastest way to make any writing experience into a chore. Starting with a meaningful, limited, specific topic can make writing a pleasant experience for you, if not a pleasure.

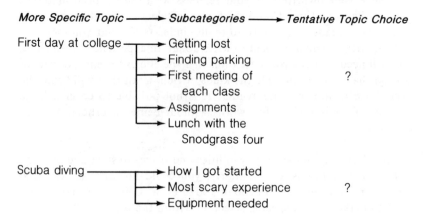

More Specific Topic ⟶ *Subcategories* ⟶ *Tentative Topic Choice*

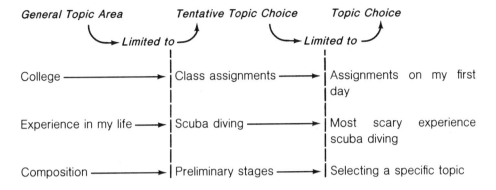

In effect, if you begin with a small topic, you will discover that the theme begins to write itself. Events come to mind; details fall into place. You will feel that you have an experience or an idea worth sharing and that you want to get started. You *want* to tell about the time you almost got killed scuba diving, even if you didn't so much like the idea of writing about an experience in your life. As you divide the "experience in your life" topic into smaller and smaller units, and as you select from among those, determining which seem intriguing and which not, deciding what it is you really want to talk about, the topic and the assignment become your own. *You* have something to say, and you are ready to get on with it.

EXERCISE 1
Analyze the following topics to determine which of them are small

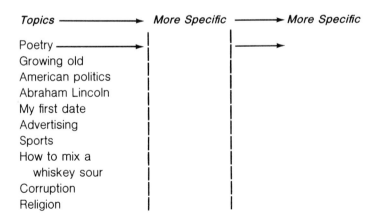

enough to serve as the focus of a 500-word theme. Subdivide those that are too big until they are small enough to be useful.

EXERCISE 2
Read the following student themes. Which develop a limited enough topic? Which do not? In your judgment are the topics selected worthy of the students' attention? How might these themes be improved? How might specific-issue lists have helped?

A

Working

My parents are among those who believe that every student should "work his way through school." Why? Because they did it that way.

While I am not against the great American "work ethic," I do believe that there is a certain amount of false logic inherent in my parents' point of view. Things which suited for their generation may not necessarily work for mine. And what they suggest did not work for everyone in their generation. I'm sure that many people even then had parents who "put them through school." Others borrowed to get an education. Not everyone "worked."

My generation faces different problems than did my parents' peer group. When they were in school, a college degree was an "open sesame" to a job. Now, only the very best people at the very best schools have that advantage from a degree—if they have it. With competition for grades and for the jobs beyond the degrees what it is, I believe that students must concentrate their entire efforts on their education and not attempt to "work their way through school." No discipline is developed from undertaking too much and failing at some of it.

B

Working

I have worked at one job or another ever since I was a small child washing neighbors' windows for pocket money. I went the gamut from baby-sitting to a paper route (still not a usual job for a girl). And I worked in the soda shop in the small town in which I grew up during my high school years.

I believe that I learned a lot from working. I learned how to get along with different kinds of people. You met just about everyone at the soda shop at one time or another. I learned that you have to be willing to serve others (no pun intended) in order to earn your way through the world. And I learned that I could manage to work and still get by in school. I earned good grades, even though I worked.

Nonetheless, I did miss a lot of the social life which comes with being a teenager. Between working afternoons and Saturdays, there wasn't much energy left for much else except schoolwork. The way things look right now, the same will be true for my college years. I have to work to eat. So I work. Yet it saddens me that I cannot afford to enjoy the things which other students have.

C

Working

Working is and always has been important in the world. Ever since people were on this earth, they have had to work in order to survive. If you think of it, even animals work for their food. They hunt.

People have traditionally undertaken many kinds of work in order to survive. There are construction and education. Religion and farming are kinds of work. And of course, there are politics and transportation. Even the military is a kind of work.

Work is truly one of the things that make men human.

D

My New Dress

The most important new dress I ever bought was the one I bought for the prom. It was extremely important to me, as you can imagine, to be beautiful for my senior prom. So I shopped carefully for days until I found just the right one.

Luckily, it worked out fine. My date thought it was the most beautiful dress he ever saw, or so he said. I was very pleased with this experience.

E

Dinner at the Rogers House

To be truthful, I cannot pinpoint one experience in my life that is most important. Maybe someday I will be able to do so. But for right now, my most important experience is really a series of experiences—a series which has lasted ever since I can remember. I am talking about our family dinner.

What makes dinner at the Rogers' home different from the experience at most other homes is the series of rules my parents developed before we were born and which they taught us as we were growing up. The rules were simple. Each dinner would be treated as something special, a time of communion and renewal. A time when family members looked at each other with the respect and courtesy shown to valued friends. A time when all gripes and grievances were to be left aside. If a family member could not abide by those rules for the evening, that member was not to come to the table. It was not a punishment, and it was not intended as one. Rather, it was a way of not spoiling it for the others. The person who could not get into the spirit of things understood it as such and really preferred it that way.

More than anything else, this pleasant time brought our family together, and really made a family out of us. When other folks were grouchy and squabbling, we were pleasant and considerate. We all knew we had this pristine time coming, which helped to make even a bad day more bearable. And we learned a kind of self-control from it, a way of not becoming emotionally involved with the unpleasant parts of the day. That is something I will take with me for the rest of my life. And I hope that I will be able to carry on this tradition when I have a family of my own.

EXERCISE 3

Select a topic for a 250- to 350-word theme. Subdivide it until you think that it is small enough to be covered in a satisfying manner in this number of words. (If you have a topic that intrigues you, you may choose to write a longer theme so that you can cover it fully.) Write a specific-issue list to check on your thinking process, and then write your theme.

2. Defining Your Audience and Purpose

Your audience is the person or persons to whom your theme or letter or other communication is addressed. Your purpose is your reason for writing that specific communication in that specific way. Both of these basic definitions are worthy of further exploration, for the success or failure of your theme or other communication may well hinge on how effectively you define your audience and your purpose.

Obviously, when you are assigned a theme your audience will be your instructor and sometimes your classmates. So you can make certain assumptions about your audience, some of which will depend on your topic as well.

You can assume that the person is literate, that he or she understands sentence structure, grammar, and most vocabulary, and has some grasp of the fundamentals of many disciplines. Even if you are writing about less common topics, this particular audience is likely to be able to follow your discussion. If, however, you will be dealing with a highly specialized or technical topic, with a hobby that requires a lot of unusual knowledge, or with something else that is really out of the ordinary, it would be well to plan to provide some background information and relevant definitions as part of your theme. You might use the introduction for this job, or you might build the information into the structure of your theme or even use a glossary of terms. Which way or ways you select for providing background data for your readers will depend on several things, including your topic and your audience. But it is vital that you provide any background information that your audience is likely to need to understand what you are saying.

Although your later themes may have several "purposes," for now you will be concentrating your attention on a single purpose: to explain your main idea as expressed by your thesis sentence as clearly and fully as you can to your assumed reader. Such a purpose might be expressed as "I intend to show that my thesis sentence concept is true."

THESIS SENTENCE: Students should have the option of passing subject tests rather than taking courses in fields outside their major.

PURPOSE STATEMENT: *I intend to show that* students should have the option of passing subject tests rather than taking courses in fields outside their major.

Generally, such a statement of purpose would *not* appear in your theme. It is simply a way of clarifying what you are doing as you write your theme. And sometimes statements of purpose will include a bit of strategy as well:

PURPOSE STATEMENT: *I intend to use humor and specific examples to show that* students should have the option of passing subject tests rather than taking courses in fields outside their majors.

Adding strategy will help you define the kinds of materials that belong in your theme and the kind of tone (*tone* is the attitude the writer takes toward the subject and audience) that you want to develop.

But your central concern as a writer and as a communicator must always be your audience. Your job as a communicator is to transfer ideas and emotions intact from your mind to the mind of another person who may not be listening and may not want to cooperate. Even a friendly reader needs to be enticed into your subject and, once drawn in, held by your commitment to what you are saying. Any skills you can use to make what you have to say clear and concise, relevant to your reader if possible, and easy to follow and understand (the format of your theme shows your commitment, as do its style and content) will make the communication process work that much more smoothly. As you may remember, this concept of audience is where your writing work started as you analyzed the effectiveness of various letter in Chapter 1. And you will return to the analysis of audience in later chapters of this book.

For now, however, let us assume a specific audience for your themes, recognizing at the same time that in the real world audiences will vary widely and such assumptions are not always easy to make. But for now, so that you may get started on your rough-draft writing, let us assume that you are writing to a person who has an open mind on most subjects, is generally willing to listen to an opposing point of view, and is reasonably willing to be interested in what you have to say if you are. We will assume that the person understands the fundamentals of sentence structure, grammar, and spelling, so that you will not have to write very "simply" but will be expected to write "correctly" in order to have your message respected. In terms of the kinds of topics you might select, let's assume that your audience has an "average" amount of knowledge. In other words, if your topic would require that your audience have a vast store of technical or unusual background information, you may have to provide some of that data as part of your theme. If you are unsure, assume that your audience knows about as much about the topic as you did when you first started looking into it, or else consult your instructor.

As you read the following student compositions, analyze them to determine whether they would succeed in communicating with the audience just described. Where, if anywhere, do they succeed well? Where do they fail? How might they be improved?

A

Our Family Business

If you never heard of "one-to-the-em spacing," and if you think that "points" have to do with scoring in a football game, if you have no idea what a "pica" is and have never heard of "secondary leading," it is a cinch that you family is not in the typesetting business. Mine has been for the last few years.

Getting type turned around for clients may not seem like a very glamorous business. It isn't. What it is is a high-pressure, last minute, uncertain kind of world where you have to be prepared to handle monumental jobs quickly and precisely with almost no notice. Of course, it would be too much to ask to have the work steady or predictable. So it is often very hard to staff or plan properly.

B

Our Family Business

We don't have a family business in the normal sense of it, but I chose this topic anyway since my brother and I had a business together during the years when we were growing up. I thought that it would be an interesting topic for discussion in this assignment.

My brother and I served as the "neighborhood garden and all purpose boys" for our neighborhood. What that means is that we mowed lawns, did windows, helped people move in (and out), waited near the grocery store to help people load packages into their cars (for tips), and in general, made ourselves useful. What was unusual about it is that our business together lasted over the course of several years. We set up a "corporation" (Right Brothers, Inc.), we had stock (we each owned 50%), and we had shareholders' meetings. The meetings were fairly small since there were only two shareholders.

The business is dissolved now—we have gone our separate ways. But, believe it or not, it generated most of the money we both needed for our college educations.

C

The Family Business

Our family is in the insulation business.

In the insulation business, R-value is a key term. We discuss R-values for insulation with our customers whenever we got out to bid on a job. Customers usually don't really know what R-value is, though they have usually heard the term before.

Another important thing is quality of workmanship. An insulation job that is not done properly might just as well not be done.

As you can tell from your reading of the first sample theme, unusual facts and names can be used as part of the interest-getting function of the introductory paragraph. The writer never really explains what "one-to-the-em spacing" is, nor does she ever return to the other technical terms. Yet, as the "average" reader, you probably do not consider this a defect in the theme. You might even be inclined to try to get further information on your own.

The third theme, on the other hand, focuses your attention on "R-value." Even though the writer says that most people have heard the term but don't know what it means, she does not bother to explain it—clearly a mistake in terms of audience analysis.

When you are writing to real-life audiences, your ability to analyze and to prepare for their reactions to what you are saying will have a critical impact on your chances of communicating successfully. In the real world your letter will very often come as an unwelcome interruption in an already miserable day. And just because you have addressed your letter to a company vice president does not mean that that person will see it first (indeed, it is unlikely that he or she will). A problem that seems urgent to you, moreover, may not seem all that critical to your audience. Thus, if you can put yourself into your audience's shoes as you write and say what you have to say from their perspective, clearly, precisely, and briefly, you have taken a big step closer to getting your point across.

EXERCISE 1

Think of an issue or subject that is important to you in your personal life. How might that issue look to a person in opposition to you, such as your parent or child or instructor? Briefly (in a paragraph or two) describe your point of view; then do the same thing for the other person. Then see whether you can tell your side of the story in the language that is least likely to trigger a hostile reaction from the other person and most likely to engender agreement, again writing a paragraph or two.

What is the difference between the paragraphs? Be prepared to discuss your analyses in class before submitting your assignment.

EXERCISE 2
Select a controversial topic that is currently under discussion in the news media. What points of view are involved? How does the issue look to each side? What is the background of the people involved? What does a person's point of view have to do with the position he or she takes on issues? Be prepared to discuss your findings in class.

3. Developing Your Thesis Sentence and Working Papers

Broadly defined, your topic is what you are writing about. Your *thesis sentence* is the single most important thing you have to say about your topic. It sets the direction for your paper. Every idea, each paragraph and sentence, and even each word must be relevant to the thesis sentence concept and must help clarify and explain it. While you may have other reasons for writing (for example, to complete the assignment), your purpose in terms of the theme itself is to explain the thesis sentence idea to your reader. Once that job is done, your theme is complete. Until that job is done, you have work to do.

Very often your thesis sentence idea and your theme topic will develop concurrently: You know that you have a topic when you discover that you have something worth saying about it.

Tentative Topic Choice	*Tentative Thesis Sentence*
Assignments on my first day at college	Assignments on my first day at college almost overwhelmed me with their scope and difficulty.
Most scary experience scuba diving	I only had one really scary experience in my five years of scuba diving as a hobby, but that one almost killed me.
My first date	If I knew for sure that all my dates would be like my first one, my first date would have been my last.

Unlike your topic choice, which may be a phrase, your thesis sentence will be a complete sentence with a properly and carefully formulated subject and predicate. You will need to make a special effort to ensure that your thesis sentence says precisely what you want it to say and not almost what you meant.

Tentative Topic Choice	Tentative (Careless) Thesis Sentence
Political corruption	All Republican (or Democratic) politicians are crooked.
Foods and fads	The "grapefruit craze" of last year was the biggest craze of all time.
Robert Frost's first poem	Robert Frost's first poem meant more to him than any other.
Napoleon	Napoleon was the world's greatest general.
The Civil War	The Civil War was the worst war in America's history.

As you read these tentative topics and thesis sentences, you probably noticed problems in both areas. "Political corruption," for example, is far too large a topic for a college theme. When the topic is too large to cover, the thesis sentence is likely to be too large as well. No one could possibly discuss "all" Republican politicians in a 500- or 1,000- or even 20,000-word theme.

The second topic, "foods and fads," is probably also too large (depending on how many "fads" there are). In this case, though, the student has limited the "foods and fads" idea in writing the thesis sentence. The "grapefruit craze" seems to be a small enough topic. The problem here is with the predicate of the sentence.

Saying that the grapefruit craze was the "biggest craze of all time" commits the student to a monumental amount of work just to discover the facts about other crazes, and then to an impossible amount of writing to describe them. Moreover, a logical exploration of past fads is likely to reveal that another "craze" was in fact more important.

What probably happened with this thesis sentence is that the student simply exaggerated a bit. In the normal give and take of a friendly conversation, that would not have mattered. But writing by nature does not allow for give and take. The reader cannot ask questions of the writer. The writer cannot gauge the reader's level of understanding or how the reader will react. Under these conditions exaggeration is a bad habit to develop. The goal of your thesis sentence is to say *precisely* what you mean—no more and no less. There are very few "all or nothing" situations that can be discussed within the constraints of a theme.

The thesis sentence about Robert Frost presents a slightly different problem. As expressed, it commits the student to coping with the feelings of a person who is no longer alive and thus is not available to be interviewed. So the theme becomes a research project.

But even if the student found a direct quotation from Frost's work to support the thesis sentence, the theme would still ring hollow. The thesis sentence misses the heart of the matter: It is "why" Robert Frost's first poem meant more to him than any other that is the center of the topic. As expressed, this thesis sentence is analogous to saying things like "I like the color red" or "Strawberries grow on vines." Once the statement has been made and accepted, little more can be said about it—unless the statement is rephrased. The student who attempted to write a theme using the Robert Frost thesis sentence as initially expressed would have a difficult time finding interesting things to say.

So the sentence must be rethought and rephrased. Why, first of all, select this aspect of the topic of discussion? Why make this assertion about it? Wouldn't something else be better or easier to write about? Perhaps what the student really means is that Robert Frost's first poem expressed a theme that occurred again and again in later poems and it is because of this repetition that we can conclude that the theme was important to him. If so, the thesis statement should be rephrased to indicate that fact.

Tentative Thesis Sentence: Robert Frost's first poem treated a theme that appeared again and again in his work.

A theme built around that thesis would spend time on several of the main instances (mentioning that others could be treated but that space did not allow for such coverage), concluding, perhaps, that the continued treatment indicates the importance of that topic to the man himself. Even though you may not know Frost's poetry well enough to write the paper, you can probably see from this much development how the paper would grow—when you can do that, you have a good indication that your thesis sentence is workable.

The thesis sentence about Napoleon does not work because it, like the sentence about politicians, commits the student to too much in the way of discussion and research. There have been too many generals and there are too many criteria for measuring "greatness" for this topic to be workable.

The more difficult the assigned topic seems to be and the less congenial, the more important it is to limit it carefully and to phrase your thesis sentence precisely so that the rest of your writing work will progress as easily as possible.

Here is how one student handled the problem of generating a topic, a thesis sentence, and a plan for writing a theme about an assigned reading selection.

General Topic: A 450–600-word theme about Barker's essay.

Specific Topic Possibilities	*Tentative Thesis Sentence*	*Development Plan*
Barker's main idea	Barker's main idea— that people have a *right* to a certain standard of living— was convincingly explained in his essay.	Work through essay sequentially, citing his examples and evidence to demonstrate truth of thesis.
His use of examples	Although compelling in themselves, Barker's examples were not really relevant to the point he was making.	Go through essay, showing that examples were poignant and demonstrating their lack of relevance to his thesis sentence.

Before doing any further work on the theme, the student would have to decide which of the thesis sentence assertions was true: It would seem that they are mutually exclusive. If Barker's main idea was convincingly explained, his examples should have also been relevant to his thesis sentence. Thus, part of the preliminary work for some themes will entail other kinds of work, such as making sure a reading assignment is understood, reviewing class notes, doing research, and so on. The composition cannot be written before the other steps are accomplished. Nonetheless, this student has shown a good understanding of how to get started on an assignment: He is exploring specific topic possibilities, trying out thesis sentences, and working on plans for the paper as a whole.

One of the ways in which you can help yourself perform your preliminary writing tasks easily and successfully is by taking a few moments to develop working papers for each assignment. If you are using specific-idea lists to help you select a workable topic, as suggested in Chapter 1, you have already started.

Working papers are practical notes to yourself, something you would not submit to an instructor (except for the purpose of having your skills evaluated). They would include your idea list, your overall and specific topic work, your thesis sentence statements, your audience analysis, and brief purpose statements for your theme. They don't have to be formal or neat. One student did it this way for the "grapefruit craze" topic:

Working Papers: Theme 2

ASSIGNMENT: Write a 400–700-word theme on the topic of your choice. Submit working papers, including idea list, and showing development of topic, thesis sentence, audience analysis and purpose.

IDEAS: Politics. Salmon fishing. Diets. Foods and fads—last year's grapefruit craze.

TOPIC: Grapefruit craze of last year.

TENTATIVE THESIS: The big grapefruit craze of last year was the biggest craze of all time.

AUDIENCE ANALYSIS: Assume audience to be "average adult"; topic does not require special background or treatment.

POSSIBLE PURPOSES: Treat tentative thesis seriously, explaining how grapefruit craze affected diets and health of people caught up in it *or* treat grapefruit craze as humor, with the purpose of making the audience laugh.

I see two theme possibilities, as follows:

Theme 2A

PURPOSE STATEMENT: My purpose for this theme is to show that the grapefruit craze of last year had a serious negative effect on the health of those people caught up in it.

THESIS SENTENCE: The big grapefruit craze of last year had a serious negative effect on the health of those people caught up in it.

Theme 2B

PURPOSE STATEMENT: My purpose for this theme is to amuse people by showing how silly fad diets are.

THESIS SENTENCE: The grapefruit craze which struck last year allowed dieters a chance to express fully and creatively their self-destructive tendencies.

You can see how working papers would be useful to you. They give you a tool with which you can explore your topic idea and your thesis sentence possibilities. When you have finished preparing your working papers, you will be well on your way to evaluating how workable your topic actually is and how likely you are to be able to develop your thesis sentence into a worthwhile discussion. The student working on the grapefruit craze paper would not have to select between approaches at this point, since he is still working on the preliminary stages of writing, but he is beginning to generate the ideas he will need to develop either theme. He can generate the ideas because he knows what he is looking for: facts, examples, data, reasons, statistics—anything, in short, to demonstrate and explain the thesis sentence to the intended audience.

Because the thesis sentence, more than anything else, will determine the direction and focus of your theme, it is crucial that you devote the necessary time and attention to phrasing it exactly. A careless exaggeration may promise an "all or nothing" discussion or a research project that you are unable or unwilling to undertake. Careful phrasing, on the other hand, will help launch you successfully into the structuring and development of the theme as a whole.

EXERCISE 1

Evaluate the following student topic and thesis sentence choices. What, if any, problems would you foresee in developing a 400- to 600-word theme about each? How would you correct those problems?

Tentative Topic Choice	Tentative Thesis Sentence
The inflation rate	The inflation rate is intolerable.
Food	Strawberries are the best-tasting food.

EXERCISE 2

Read the following student paragraphs, underlining the main sentence. Which paragraphs develop their main sentences? Which wander away from it? Which seem to have no main sentence at all? Be prepared to defend your conclusions in class.

A

Professional football consumes far too much of the nation's time and money. Each season, millions of people spend hundreds of millions of hours and hundreds of millions of dollars on professional football. Consider not only the husbands locked in front of the televisions, but the costs of buying tickets. Consider too the related costs, beer, pretzels, parking, parking tickets. And then there is the time and money spent preparing boys to become football players.

B

My hobby is art. I like to go to museums and observe the works of the master painters. I like to collect prints of my favorite paintings. I have always liked art, ever since my mother introduced me to it. Her mother was a famous artist so she grew up with it too.

C

Sandra was the most interesting person at the party. We arrived early because it looked like rain and we didn't want to get wet. She did not come until later. The party was pretty good, though, because everyone had a good time together.

D

To me, not too many things are worth fighting about. But one is the word *girl*. I have not been a "girl" for some years now, but men continue to refer to me as one. As in, "Hi, girls, how are you." I find it very demeaning.

EXERCISE 3

Assume that you have been asked to write a theme of 250 to 500 words about your first day at college. List ten possibilities for a more specific topic.

Select four of the most promising of those possibilities and subdivide each until you have what you think would be a specific, worthwhile discussion topic in each of the four categories. Develop a thesis sentence that precisely expresses your major idea about each one. Submit your working papers to your instructor along with your four specific topics and thesis sentences.

EXERCISE 4

This year you have decided to try out for a position on your college's newspaper or magazine. The editor has just asked you to prepare a 500-word article on student rights as your "tryout." What problems are you going to face as you try to develop the article?

Use working papers to solve the topic problems you foresee. Include your idea list, audience analysis, tentative smaller topics, thesis sentence possibilities, and purpose statements as part of your working papers. Submit your working papers to your instructor, and be prepared to discuss this assignment in class.

EXERCISE 5

Read the following student themes, paying special attention to the way in which the themes develop and explain the idea expressed by the thesis sentence. Which themes have topics that are too big, too abstract, or too vague? Which develop the thesis sentence idea clearly and fully? (The thesis sentence in each theme is in italics.) Be prepared to discuss these themes in class.

A

Students should have all the rights and privileges that their parents expect for themselves. If you are old enough to go to war and fight for your country, you should be old enough to buy a beer in the corner tavern. If you are old enough to get married, you ought to be able to determine your own code of dress. Even if you must live at home for one reason or another, your parents should still treat you as an adult, for it is a fact that you are an adult by any measure except economics.

In this country, it is very hard for people under the age of 21 to support themselves and go to college at the same time. The economics of the system are against younger people. No matter how talented you are, it is hard for you to get a good job without years of experience. And of course, you can't get the experience without first having the job. So the student is faced with the problem of having to go to school full time and work long part time hours for low pay, or to reverse it and work long full time hours for low pay and go to school longer. In either case, the student winds up with a very little bit of money for his or her trouble and cannot easily maintain a home. Thus the student is forced to live with parents and be treated like a child when really it is the economic system that is at fault.

B

If it is true that fat people are not jolly—and by and large it is true that fat people are not jolly—it is because skinny and average and previously fat people look at those of us of the rotund persuasion with something resembling a cross between pity and scorn. I myself have always been somewhat more than slender. That is because I enjoy eating. And while I believe in the value of exercise, I don't enjoy exercising. So I eat more than I exercise. It is that simple.

What I do not understand is what possible business it is of anyone else if I weigh more than the "norm." Why should I be subject to suggestions for "self-improvement" from complete strangers or incomplete friends? If they were complete friends, you know, they would accept me as I am. I accept them, and don't offer suggestions unasked. As long as I am happy as I am, they should be happy for me.

But happy they are not. In the fact that I indulge my craving for a chocolate sundae or a helping of French fries, I challenge their insecure egos. They retaliate by pitying me, poor soul that I am, or by scorning my lack of self-control. But I ask you, how can they evaluate the status of my "self" control? If I prefer as a rational and considered decision to be flfteen pounds the heavier and not *always* preoccupied with the latest diet and not *always* miserable because I can't stay on it, who is to say that my self-control or my point of view, either one, is at fault? Perhaps fat people would be jolly if the rest of the world were a little happier. And perhaps everyone else would be a little happier if they broke down and ate what they wanted. Chocolate éclair, anyone?

C

No advertising should be allowed on television shows geared for children under the age of eight or nine years. Children younger than this have no rational basis on which to evaluate the promises made by advertisements. They see a toy and want it, especially when advertisers use all the "tricks" at their command to sell the toy to the children. Or else they see a food item and want that. The only way the children have of getting what they want is pestering their parents for it. Often the item is not good for the children anyway and the parents refuse or punish the children for asking. There is no point to having advertising on shows for very young children. Let the toy manufacturers display their products on adult shows so that parents may make the decision for their children. In that way, manufacturers still sell products, and children can be protected until they are old enough to protect themselves.

EXERCISE 6
Select a topic in consultation with your instructor for a 300- to 600-word theme. Narrow the topic until you have a small yet significant issue to discuss. Formulate a thesis sentence and list ideas to explain and develop it. Make sure your ideas are both specific and relevant. Organize them so that they make sense to you, and write the theme.

chapter 3

generating and evaluating ideas

1. Generating Ideas for Your Themes

Stop to consider it and you will be amazed to realize that you already know an extraordinary number of things and in great detail. You have been hundreds of places and had innumerable experiences. A dozen people have probably loved you in one way or another, and many more have irritated you and infuriated you and calmed you down. Of course, you have had these effects on other people. You have probably worked at a job or two, and you have certainly spent years in school. Why, then, would you *ever* have to struggle to find a topic to write about or for things to say once you have the topic?

At one time or another, almost every writer is stuck for ideas. If that happens to you, it just means that you are experiencing a normal part of life, not that you "can't write" or that you can't write about a specific topic. There are a number of common reasons that people have difficulty handling a writing topic: They don't understand what is wanted or they don't fully understand something else like a reading assignment, or they haven't devoted enough time to the prewriting process before they sit down to work. The solutions to these problems are obvious.

Other times people can't get started because the topic isn't initially congenial to them or they don't know enough about it to have anything to say. Learning a little more about the topic will help get you started. Encyclopedias, including children's encyclopedias, which have clear, often illustrated explanations, and casebooks, which are collections of essays on a given topic such as civil rights, and other sources on your library reference shelves can provide you with reliable information on most topics very quickly. But it is usually a mistake to begin "taking notes" before you have a good idea of your topic and thesis sentence. Otherwise, you are likely to be taking notes almost forever on background information that you may never use and that may in fact get in your way because you feel that you "should" use it. At this point you should be taking notes *only* on potential topics, thesis sentences, and major ideas for your theme's development. It is helpful to write only on one side of the page so that you can "cut and paste" later. And it is necessary to keep track of your sources so that you can quote them properly and correctly and so that you are sure which ideas belong to your sources and which are your own.

Sometimes a quick review of your textbooks or notes will be the best place to get an idea. If nothing else works, though, you will just have to get started somewhere, anywhere, as long as you get started.

Suppose, for example, that you must write a 500- to 700-word theme on a topic of your choice. You can think of nothing except that you are not feeling too well because you ate too much spaghetti at dinner. But you must get started on the theme. So you start with spaghetti—or with overeating, for that matter.

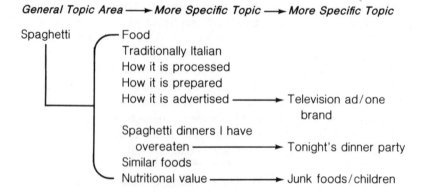

If you get started—somewhere—and use the process you have learned to break general topic areas into specific topics, you can locate a worthwhile discussion topic in a few moments. You might decide to write about how junk foods are advertised on television or how spaghetti came to be the main course for tonight's dinner party, or you might get absolutely nowhere in your discussion of spaghetti. But—and this is important—the point is that you have gotten started. Writing is a process of discovery—you find out what you really have to say about a topic as you write. You locate a topic by starting somewhere and working from there.

Other times you have a topic and can think of nothing more to say to fill up the several hundred words left to write. This problem too can be overcome.

Begin by evaluating your topic. The likelihood is that the topic is too broad or too vague or too abstract, and needs to be further subdivided—even if that sounds wrong. It would seem that you should have more to say about a big topic than a small one, but in fact that is not true. A topic like "Abraham Lincoln" or "the Civil War" leads you in so many directions at the same time and requires so much commentary on so many concepts that you won't know where to start or stop or how to hold your discussion together. If your topic is like this, you will need to subdivide it.

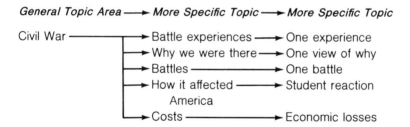

Even the most specific topics in this chart may be too large to cover properly in a short discussion. You may have to focus your attention on the most critical hour of that one experience of the war, or on student reaction at one place on one day. Otherwise, your theme will stay on the surface of your knowledge and opinions, or you will be so overwhelmed by the topic that you can't think of anything to say at all. As a beginning writer, you are far more likely to select a topic that is too big to handle than one that is too small. That is the first thing to think of if you find that you have "nothing to say" and words yet to write.

Sometimes your problem is not with your topic but with the amount of information you have. On any topic, but especially on an assigned topic that is unfamiliar to you, you may need to do some research to gather enough facts to fill out your composition. A theme can use examples and data of various sorts (statistics, reports of research, facts) and reasons and anecdotes. There are many things to say to support a specific point. You will learn how to write paragraphs using each of these items in a later chapter. But you can generate ideas (or idea slots, which you will fill with facts in the course of your research) simply and easily by using a table very much like the multiplication tables you studied when you were a child. You can use this method either to select a topic that you are sure you can discuss (because you will be able to get the information you need to fill your theme) or to develop information for a topic that you must discuss.

The table is easy to make. Simply place discussion topics across the top and discussion categories down the side as shown in Table 1.

TABLE 1

	Ford	*Chevrolet*	*Oldsmobile*
Purchase cost			
Maintenance			
Reliability			
Styles			
Mileage			
Insurance			
Other			

For this discussion you might need a table several pages long so that you could say something about the purchase cost of each kind of car in the appropriate block, about the maintenance, and so on. And you would probably want to use the various models of Ford, or some of them, and the various models of Chevrolet, and so on. After you have made your table, you could decide to compare one Ford model, one Chevrolet, and one Oldsmobile with approximately the same cost in terms of other categories. (Thesis sentence: Although these three cars cost approximately the same amount, the Ford is clearly the best selection in terms of reliability, miles per gallon, and other service aspects.) Or you might decide to discuss one model in terms of the various categories. (Thesis sentence: The new Chevrolet for this year appears to be an extraordinary value in terms of low cost, high reliability, and ease of service.) If you need more to say to fill your theme, you can add another discussion category (availability of special options, for example) or another example or two in an existing category.

You can use the same technique for difficult or abstract topics assigned to you. For example, if you must discuss several poets or philosophies or if you must select one poem or philosophy to discuss, you can set up a table like Table 2.

TABLE 2

	Shelley	*Wordsworth*	*Byron*
Theme			
Plot			
Characters			
Diction			
Relationships			

You would find something to say about the themes of Shelley's poetry (or one or two of his poems) and about the themes of Wordsworth's poetry and Byron's. You could then compare their themes. Or you could work down Table 2, talking about Shelley's poems (or a specific poem) in terms of one or several of the discussion categories. The categories and information for an assignment like this would have to come from your readings and notes. And you will undoubtedly have to limit your topic to one (or at the most two) poems or issues.

Similar tables can be used to help you complete assignments in other classes, whether you must cope with the history of philosophy, great plays, or even a comparative study of the development of the rules for baseball, football, and soccer. And you could use such a table in real life to help you as you attempt to compare choices among houses or apartments, insurance policies, bank loans, or almost any issue that might come to mind. The fact is that you can generate ideas and discussion topics for almost any topic at all if you know how to do it and are willing to try.

EXERCISE 1

Many of your writing assignments in composition courses and in other courses, such as history, philosophy, sociology, economics, psychology, and so on, will require you to be able to deal with large and complicated topics. Your first job, in all likelihood, will be to learn something about that topic so that you can begin to make good topic subdivision choices. The obvious place to start your learning is with the textbooks for that course.

However, in many cases the texts will not be enough. That is when the reference section of your library can be invaluable to you *if* you know how to use it. The purpose of this assignment is to help you get used to the reference section of your library so that you can use it quickly and effectively.

Select four of the topics listed for a "research project." Your reference librarian may help you get started in your search for the sources that will provide you with clear, quick, useful information. It is a good idea to keep track of those sources for future use (you might want to set up an index card file listing the name, call number, and kind of material available in each one). Then check the library card catalog in the main section of your library to see what is listed. Jot down several of the more promising titles, and then check the shelves to see which books are actually available. Examine the books themselves to see which have indexes and glossaries to help you get to the information you need quickly. Now is also a good time to investigate your library's procedures for searching for "missing" books and recalling overdue books from other users when you need them for a project. Some libraries do these things very quickly, while others are not reliable about such matters.

Finally, check the library's magazine reference section, if it has one, to find out what kinds of current information are available to you.

TOPICS

1. Colley Cibber
2. Anthropomorphism
3. Knute Rockne
4. The acid test ratio
5. The Bacon–Shakespeare controversy
6. The "big bang" theory
7. *Carpe diem*
8. Nihilism
9. The Pushtunistan dispute
10. Cubism

EXERCISE 2

You can use a table to help you cope with the information you gather on complex topics as well as to help you generate ideas and develop organizational patterns. For example, suppose you have been asked to write a 500- to 750-word theme about corporate finance. You have limited that topic to "reading and understanding financial statements." Your table might look something like Table 3 as you have begun to organize your ideas.

TABLE 3

	Purpose	Contents	Meaning
1. Income Account			
2. Balance sheet			
3. Supplemental			
4. Annual report			

As you worked more with your topic and started to fill in your chart, you would realize that you had far too much material to cover in a 750-word theme; your chart itself would tell you that because it would get very, very full. You might decide that you really wanted to focus on one aspect of the annual report or of the balance sheet and its relationship to corporate finance, or you might decide to discuss a common thread, such as an accounting principle. However you subdivided your topic, though, you could still make another chart to help you generate and organize ideas and control the writing process.

Assume that you have been asked to write a 500- to 750-word theme on one of these complex topics. Subdivide it until it is small enough to be handled (you may need to do some quick library research first), and write a thesis sentence for a potential theme. Then set up a chart to help you develop discussion categories and ideas. Fill in the chart with data from your own experience or quick library research on the subject, or, prepare a specific-issue list from which you could write the theme.

TOPICS

1. Philosophy
2. Modern theatre
3. Plays by William Shakespeare
4. The job market in your chosen field
5. Sibling rivalry
6. Economics

2. Evaluating Arguments and Points of View

Part of learning how to write an effective theme is developing your ability to analyze ideas and facts objectively. Ideas, and even "facts," sometimes can be fairly complicated, and "the truth" may not be easy to discern. Each person sees from a particular and special perspective, which is one reason that people often have difficulty agreeing on exactly what happened in a given situation. People remember differently as well. Certain elements of an event or discussion fit more closely into a person's previous experience and thought patterns, and it is these that tend to be remembered. If you've ever been in a class on a totally new subject, you can relate to this experience. At first, everything in the lecture or discussion seems strange and you have difficulty remembering anything at all; study is laborious. After a while, though, the words and concepts become more familiar to you; it is easier to follow the discussion because you already have a network of ideas to serve as background.

Up to this point in your writing experience, you have been asked to prepare expository themes—themes in which your goal has been to get your reader to say, "I understand your point of view." If the reader really understands, there is likely to be little dispute with what you are saying—assuming that your facts are correct. For example, once your reader understood your problem with the bus schedules (buses that should make connections in fact did not), that person would be very likely to agree with your judgment. And you will still be writing compositions that ask you to explain a point of view clearly and effectively.

But in your college writing classes, and in "real-world" writing situations, you will also have to handle topics about which reasonable people disagree. Like expository topics, these writing assignments come in small and jumbo sizes, from whether or not the school should have a subsidized remedial-studies program to whether or not abortion should be legal in this country. These "argumentative" themes provide you with the goal of getting your reader to say, "I understand your point of view and I agree" or, if that is not possible (and it often is not), "I understand the merits of your position."

This kind of writing will require that you apply everything you have learned about explaining your ideas. You cannot assume that your reader knows something just because you do or will follow a particular logical pathway because you did. You have to make your points and your paths explicit.

And in order to write an effective argumentative theme you must explore alternate points of view to those that you have always held. Perhaps the position you are taking is not the strongest; perhaps the opposition's point of view has merit after all.

One way to examine the merits of alternative points of view is to try to develop "both" sides of an argument (there are often several sides to develop), examining the pros and cons for each side.

Suppose, for example, that you and your cousin who lives in another state have gotten into a disagreement about whether or not there should be required courses at your respective colleges. You believe that there should not be required courses outside your major field of study, while your cousin believes in and is arguing for those courses. You have just gotten a letter from your cousin and are writing your reply using the process you have learned for writing effective themes: You think about your topic, gather your ideas, and phrase several possible thesis sentences.

THESIS STATEMENT: All courses not in a major field of study should be electives.

THESIS STATEMENT: No student should be required to take any courses outside of that student's major field of study.

THESIS STATEMENT: General requirements should be eliminated.

SUPPORTING IDEAS

1. Many courses are not relevant to anything.
2. Time could be better spent in field of major studies.
3. Competition with people majoring in other fields could lower your grade point average, thus harming your career prospects.
4. This concept could be satisfied by allowing students to select electives from other fields of study.

You would continue to list your ideas and to develop thesis statements until you were reasonably satisfied that your list was complete and accurate and that you had a thesis statement that focused the discussion correctly for you. This is pretty much the same process that you followed in your discussion of bus schedules. What is different is that now you are going to try to develop the opposition's point of view into a convincing argument. In this way you will be able to determine the strengths and weaknesses of both positions.

Often, making pro and con tables, like Table 4, will help you try out both sides of an argument. First you take your own position, list your major arguments for it, and try to counter them. For example, argument number one in the "Pro" column would be answered by argument number one in the "Con" column.

TABLE 4

Pro (Me)	Con
General Requirements Eliminated	*General Requirements Retained*
1. Many courses are not relevant to anything students do.	1. Students may not see the relevance now. Some breadth requirements are necessary in a free society.
2. Time could be better spent in field of major studies	2. Other studies are also useful; students may change major.
3. Competition with majors may reduce grade point average, thus hurting the students' career prospects.	3. Pass/fail courses can be introduced. Separate courses for non-majors could be added.
4. This concept could be satisfied through electives.	4. Students may not make the wisest choices.

Once you have understood your own position and how its major arguments might be countered, you are ready to develop the opposition's major points.

THESIS STATEMENT: General requirements are necessary.

SUPPORTING IDEAS

1. All people need certain skills (math, writing), whether they seem relevant to a career path or not.
2. A democratic society requires that people be educated in such fields as history and political science, whether those fields are interesting or relevant to a career or not, so that they may make informed decisions on the issues of our time.
3. Not all students are informed enough to select electives that are in their best interests. Students need to rely on the wisdom and experience of educators to plan their studies for them, although leeway should be allowed for a certain number of electives.

Then you can construct a table, such as Table 5, countering the opposition's major points:

TABLE 5

Pro	Con (My Position)
General Requirements Retained	*General Requirements Eliminated*
1. Required courses in non-majors fields teach necessary skills.	1. No one learns anything if he or she is not interested.
2. A democratic society requires people to have certain skills.	2. Same answer as above.
3. Students need the wisdom of educators to select their study paths.	3. Fifty years old is not necessarily fifty years' wise; students are in the best position to analyze their own needs, perhaps with the assistance of educators.

Once you have completed this table-making process, you are ready to develop a theme that focuses on the strongest of your own arguments *yet* deals effectively with the arguments and rejoinders your opponent might make.

SPECIFIC ISSUE: No student should be required to take any courses outside his or her career field (electives can be used to fill desirable objectives of general requirements).

1. Most general requirements are not "relevant" to anything a student will ever need or use. Philosophy is a fine study if you are interested, but if not, it is a waste of time and you will not really learn anyway. Genuine learning requires commitment from the student. If you are interested, you can elect to study the subject.
2. Even general requirements that might be useful, such as composition courses, cannot be taught to an uninterested, resentful student. Students who are forced to take courses do not make the most of them.
3. General requirements are actually damaging to the student because they force competition with students who are majoring in the field and because they take time that could be better spent studying major subjects. Pass/fail courses would help, but do not exist on this campus. Even pass/fail courses take time and effort.
4. Students should be allowed to select courses outside their major fields of study, to take them on a pass/fail basis, and to take them at the time of their choice.

While you may not want to follow the pro/con chart process for all the themes you write, it will be useful to you when the issue is important and the opposition strong. You will, however, want to apply your understanding of logic each and every time you set pen to paper.

Logic may be defined as a set of rules that govern those thought processes that solve problems. It plays a part, not always the major part, in all arguments. It shares the stage with emotional appeals of various sorts, which you will read about in a few moments, and, too often, with faulty logic as well. By nature people are emotional as well as logical, so that emotional appeals will at times be more convincing than logical ones. And people are often careless, which means that faulty logic can go unnoticed.

Logic is divided into two major categories, depending on how the conclusions (the results of the train of thought) are drawn. When you use *deductive* logic, you begin with a general principle that you already know is true. For instance, you know that if you are holding something in your hand and you let go, the thing will fall. If you apply that principle to a specific case—to this book, for example—you are using deductive logic.

You use *inductive* logic, the other major kind, when you don't know what general principle applies and you make deliberate tests and observations to find out. From the results of these tests and observations, you draw general conclusions, which are then available for you to use deductively. If you did not know what happened when you dropped something and if you made tests to find out, you would be using inductive logic. If you did a survey to find out whether people believe a certain idea, you would be using inductive logic in that you would be testing to find out. When you do research on a topic to learn about it, you are following a kind of inductive process.

Common sense will tell you that a proper testing procedure requires that you gather enough facts, that you gather the relevant facts, and that you draw the right conclusions. For example, it would be silly to draw a conclusion about the opinions of American students from a survey that included only ten people on your campus. If you survey enough people and don't ask the right questions, you still won't have the evidence you need. And drawing the right conclusions from the evidence at hand requires some knowledge of the *syllogism,* the major tool of deductive logic.

A syllogism is a way of testing a specific instance to see whether it fits a general principle that you already know to be true.

GENERAL PRINCIPLE: All men are mortal.

SPECIFIC INSTANCE: Socrates is a man.

CONCLUSION: Socrates is mortal.

In the language of logic, the general principle is called the *major premise* and the specific instance is called the *minor premise*.

MAJOR PREMISE: All men are mortal.

MINOR PREMISE: Socrates is a man.

CONCLUSION: Socrates is mortal.

The syllogism acts as a chain of reasoning, connecting the general principle, which we know is true, to the specific instance being tested to the conclusion that is drawn. For it to be a logically correct chain (that is, to be *valid*), certain rules must be followed.

First, the major premise must be an all-encompassing statement. If the major premise were "Some men are mortal," we would not have enough information to know whether or not Socrates would die. As long as the major premise is all-encompassing in its meaning, however, the word *all* need not be present. It is interesting to note that, for the purposes of a syllogism, a completely negative major premise is acceptable: "No men are mortal" gives you enough information to decide Socrates' fate.

Because the major premise of a syllogism is stated so definitely, it is easy for the chain of logic to break down at the start. If the major premise is faulty—for example, "All mammals are cold-blooded"—the rest of the argument cannot be correct—even if the syllogism is formed properly.

MAJOR PREMISE: All mammals are cold-blooded.

MINOR PREMISE: A rabbit is a mammal.

CONCLUSION: A rabbit is cold-blooded.

This perfectly valid chain of reasoning is not correct because the major premise itself is not factual (that is, the syllogism is valid but not true). In this sense a syllogism is like a theme: If the thesis statement is false, the best writing won't make the theme correct.

The second element in forming a valid syllogism has to do with the relationships among the premises and the conclusion.

MAJOR PREMISE: All MEN are *mortal.*

MINOR PREMISE: Socrates is a MAN.

CONCLUSION: Socrates is *mortal.*

The last term in the minor premise (MAN) must be a subcategory of the first term of the major premise (MEN). The last term in the major premise (*mortal*) must be the same as the last term in the conclusion (*mortal*). And the first term in the minor premise (Socrates) must be the same as the first term in the conclusion (Socrates).

That may seem very complicated and hard to remember, but you really don't have to remember it if you apply your common sense as you read syllogisms (and themes and arguments as well). For example, see if you can discern the problems with the following syllogisms:

1

MAJOR PREMISE: All rabbits are warm-blooded.

MINOR PREMISE: Bambi is a fawn.

CONCLUSION: Bambi is warm-blooded.

2

MAJOR PREMISE: All birds have wings.

MINOR PREMISE: An eagle is a bird.

CONCLUSION: An eagle can fly.

3

MAJOR PREMISE: Fire is hot and can burn you.

MINOR PREMISE: Ice is cold.

CONCLUSION: Ice is not hot and can't burn you.

The problem with the first syllogism is fairly obvious. The general principle applies to rabbits; if Bambi is not a rabbit, then the specific instance does not relate to the general principle and no test is possible. The mistake is here:

MAJOR PREMISE: All RABBITS are warm-blooded.

MINOR PREMISE: Bambi is a FAWN.

CONCLUSION: Bambi is warm-blooded.

While it may be *true* that fawns are also warm-blooded, that fact or conclusion cannot be drawn from this logical chain.

The second and third syllogisms have structural problems as well, even though their facts may be correct.

MAJOR PREMISE: All birds have WINGS.

MINOR PREMISE: An eagle is a bird.

CONCLUSION: An eagle CAN FLY.

It may or may not be true that having wings means that you can fly, but that is not the correct conclusion for the syllogism (which would be "An eagle has wings").

MAJOR PREMISE: FIRE is hot and can burn you.

MINOR PREMISE: ICE is cold.

CONCLUSION: Ice is not hot and can't burn you.

In this case, no matter how true or false the facts, the minor premise is not a category of the major premise and so no test is possible. The logical term for an argument that moves in this fashion is *non sequitur,* which is Latin for "it does not follow."

As you examine your own themes and the arguments of others, you will want to pay close attention to the way in which the argument is made. Is the major idea (the thesis sentence) true? If not, why not? Does the evidence being given to demonstrate the truth of the thesis sentence in fact relate to the thesis sentence, or are you in a "fire and ice" situation, with irrelevant if intriguing data? As you read the following student themes, try to determine whether the evidence is presented logically.

A

Government laws regarding the minimum wage are intended to help the poor and jobless and have exactly that effect. While it is true that a person might not be able to support a family on $2.25 per hour, or whatever the current minimum happens to be, still, that amount of money is better than nothing, and from the perspective of a proud man, better than welfare.

Leaving aside for a moment the problem of supporting a family, let us look at the problem of teenage unemployment. There are many teenagers who would be willing, in fact, very willing, to work for $2.25 per hour in order to get the money they need to buy what they want. They are not supporting a family at the moment, but they most certainly are looking for a meaningful way of filling their time, for a way of learning a job skill, and for a means of earning some pocket cash. If an employer is faced with the prospect of paying a minimum wage *and* paying social security *and* carrying insurance *and* complying with a lot of other government rigamarole, then a lot of teenagers who otherwise might find jobs will be out of work. It seems clear to me that if you don't want to work for the salary offered you don't take the job.

B

Government laws regarding the minimum wage are intended to and do in fact help the poor and jobless by preventing people with money and power (employers) from enslaving those who have neither.

If all employers could pay "what the market would bear," they would, acting in their own selfish interests, pay as little as possible. A buck in the employee's pocket is a buck out of their own. The person who is out of work and sees no other choice might be inclined or forced for that matter to take the first job available, no matter what the salary. If that salary is not a "living wage," then the employee's condition is in no way improved.

C

No matter how much good they may seem to do, a closer examination of the effects of minimum wage laws will show that they actually harm the people they are intended to help.

First, minimum wage laws never actually provide enough money for the worker to live on. The worker who is forced to survive on minimum wages thus will never escape poverty, in effect, a *minimum* life style.

Second, minimum wage laws have the effect of legislating what should be a marketplace decision. If there were no minimum, people might actually get paid *more* as employers sought to hold good workers. People would have the incentive to become good workers to earn more money.

Last, minimum wage laws are expensive to administer, requiring a plethora of government workers at all levels. This costs money which could better be spent in programs which actually help the poor such as education and upward mobility training centers.

D

Whether they do good or harm, government laws regarding the minimum wage are an inappropriate abridgement of our freedoms in the free market concept of American society. It is true that some people are protected by the laws sometimes; it is equally true that others are injured by being unable to find work because the employer is "priced out" of the market. But this is not relevant to the larger issue.

A free society requires that the people be allowed to make *all* choices which do not interfere with the rights of others. If I as an employer want to offer you a job at a salary which you consider ridiculous, then you don't take the job. If, as an employer, I wish to attract and hold good workers, I offer more money. If workers find that employers don't offer a living wage, they form unions. In short, there are other and more appropriate ways of solving the "minimum wage" problem, if it exits, than having a series of cumbersome government laws which must be administered by bureaucrats at taxpayers' expense.

Each of these student themes takes a slightly different approach to the subject. The first two argue for a minimum wage, the third against it; the fourth argues that minimum wage laws are not the way to solve the problem—if a problem exists.

It is interesting to note that the four themes used some of the same facts. For example, several students argued that a person who needs work might be forced to take the first available job, yet came to very different conclusions about the importance of this and other facts and how they affect the "solution" that each student had in mind. What made each of these themes fairly successful as an argument, however, was that each student did in fact have a solution in mind and used specific evidence in an attempt to show that his or her solution was a good one. Each student stuck to the topic and to a single point of view about it; each one organized ideas into a pattern that a reader could follow easily, and each kept the evidence subordinated, using it to demonstrate the truth of the thesis rather than allowing the evidence to lead the essay into irrelevant, if intriguing, side topics.

In many situations, though not in all, it is also acceptable to present a topic from a personal point of view. You may find it easier to write such a theme, since you will be relying on personal experience, but you will have to be careful to keep your reader and topic in mind. Consider the following theme:

E

If you've ever been seventeen, inexperienced, and looking for a job, you know what it is like to be discouraged. At one place after another, the answer is the same. They have everyone they need or can't afford to hire. After this happened to me several times, I began to investigate the cause, and found it to be something called the "minimum wage law."

As the business people explained it to me, the government has a great number of regulations which constrain what businesses can and can't do. For example, a business cannot say that it needs 20 hours' worth of work and has $40 dollars to invest—because, in the judgment of Uncle Sam, that amount of money is not enough to pay someone for working that number of hours.

It seems to me that how much is "enough" depends on a lot of things, including the kind of work being done and the experience of the person doing it. A dangerous job or a very unpleasant one or one which requires a lot of experience to do should pay a higher salary than an easy, pleasant job. But the government has decreed that I can't spend 20 hours of my time selling candy in a drugstore because the pay is below the minimum wage. It is clear that the minimum wage laws, no matter how well intentioned, often do more harm than good. This was true in my case.

Very often, arguments use a technique called *emotional appeal* to avoid logical discussion, hide faulty logic, or enhance the effectiveness (or so the writer thinks) of an otherwise logical theme. Emotional appeals range from deliberate lying or name calling to inviting the reader to "get on the bandwagon" to the use of testimonials from athletes or other celebrities. And often they sidestep the main point by transferring attention elsewhere, focusing on generalities that are so broad as to have no meaning, or using humor to divert attention.

What emotional appeals can you recognize in this student theme?

F

Richard Walker's position on the course which this student council should take makes no sense to me for three major reasons. First, as we all know, Walker has in the past been known to tell less than the complete truth to this assembled group, to wit, his position on faculty tenure. And, more important, Walker has been known to take faculty positions as his own. Not that I am making any accusations. You see the facts. You can judge for yourself.

Second, as everyone with any sense already knows, the students on this campus will not stand for a council that goes along with Walker's position on academic freedom. If the faculty has the freedom to say and publish what it wants, the students should have that freedom too. So I respectfully suggest that you get with the opinion of the students before the students get themselves new leaders.

Finally, I want you to know that I took a little informal survey of my own, just to gauge how this vote is going to go. It is the position I suggest—that students have identical freedoms with faculty—that is going to carry in any case. So you might as well get on the winning side. With me. Against Walker.

While emotional appeals are sometimes effective in that they convince the reader or listener, they often backfire. Nobody likes to be tricked, and that in essence is what an emotional appeal does. And emotional appeals tend to lead away from the discussion of the main argument. If the student arguing against Walker had emphasized the validity of his own position and left Walker's personality out of his argument, he might have made a much stronger case for his side.

EXERCISE 1

Think of a "real-life" situation about which you hold an argumentative point of view. It may be an issue that is current on campus, something in the news, or an opinion that has been important to you for many years. But it must be argumentative; that is, the topic is not simply a matter of making someone understand a problem or situation but a matter of defending one perspective when others may also have merit.

Define your point of view on the issue by writing a thesis sentence. List the major arguments for your side; then, using a pro/con chart, try to refute those arguments. Follow the same procedure, this time defending the opposing point of view.

Select the side that, according to a logical and dispassionate analysis, is the stronger. In defense of that point of view, write either a 300- to 700-word theme or a persuasive letter of about 500 words addressed to an audience specified in your working papers.

Submit your theme or letter, the argument lists and pro/con charts you developed in preparation for writing.

EXERCISE 2

Reread the student themes about the minimum wage laws. As you do so, evaluate the kinds of evidence each student used. Which theme seems most convincing to you?

You may have noticed that these themes hardly dealt with points of view different from those the students themselves held. For the most part each theme concentrated solely on defending one side of an issue. The arguments would have been much more convincing if each student had refuted major opposing points as part of the development of his or her own theme.

Develop pro/con charts that list and refute the major arguments for all sides of the minimum wage issue. Select the point of view that seems most correct to you and write a 400- to 700-word argumentative theme defending it. Be sure to refute major opposing viewpoints as your present your own.

You may want to select a personal style for this theme, telling about your own experiences with the minimum wage law. In this case it is all right to invent experiences to exemplify your points.

EXERCISE 3

Select one of the following topics for an argumentative theme of approximately 300 to 500 words (you may have to limit the topic you choose). Define your point of view on the issue by writing a thesis sentence and listing your major arguments. Use a pro/con chart to develop your ideas. Follow the same procedure, this time defending the opposing point of view.

Select the stronger side of the argument and write a short deductive theme defending it. Then rearrange your information (you may have to alter some or add some), and prepare an inductive presentation.

TOPICS

1. Both men and women should be drafted (should not be drafted).
2. America's President should serve one six-year term.
3. College faculty should not have tenure (should have tenure).
4. College students should grade faculty performance (should not grade faculty performance).

EXERCISE 4

Select an argumentative position on an issue (it may be one you have used in a previous exercise) and present it, using emotional appeals. You may want to play on your reader's sympathy ("Hire me, because if you don't, my children will starve"), or you may want to refute your opposition by name calling or testimonials or slanting the argument in some other way. You may want to make broad, general promises that have very little meaning because they are so vague. Do anything, in fact, other than make a logical, straightforward presentation of your point of view. You may prefer to write a theme, a letter, or a speech for this assignment. Plan on approximately 500 words.

chapter 4

the structure of your theme

1. Fitting Your Theme Together

Just like letters, themes have a basic and predictable structure, with each part playing a useful role in the communication process. As with letters, the structures of themes will vary depending on content, circumstances, and audience. Understanding how the parts of themes fit together will help you get started efficiently and proceed smoothly through the theme writing process. (See Figure 2.)

In effect, your theme is the part of your letter that says what you have to say, with the framework omitted or handled elsewhere (such as on a title page). (See Figure 3.)

If you thought of your theme as a *structure,* you would probably visualize something resembling a set of blocks stacked one on top of the other, as shown in Figure 4. In this conception of a theme, each block represents one paragraph—there would not necessarily have to be five.

If you considered your composition in terms of its structural parts—the introduction (including the thesis sentence), the development, and the conclusion—the diagram would look like Figure 5. You would be planning to begin your rough draft with your thesis sentence, saving for later the job of writing a few "introductory" sentences.

While this visualization of a theme is not wrong in the sense of being an incorrect answer, it is *not* the most helpful way of looking at what

69

you will be doing as a writer. For you, the writer, and for the person who will be reading your theme, what you are building more closely resembles a ladder or stairway. Your thesis sentence places the ladder somewhere: It specifically delineates a topic and your main point about that topic. With the direction set in this manner, the paragraphs and their main sentences, the topic sentences, form the steps or rungs that take the reader on the journey through your ideas. (See Figure 6.) You may prefer to visualize your theme as a series of paragraph blocks suspended from and connected to the thesis sentence, as shown in Figure 7.

In fact, this conception of a theme as ideas expressed and under-

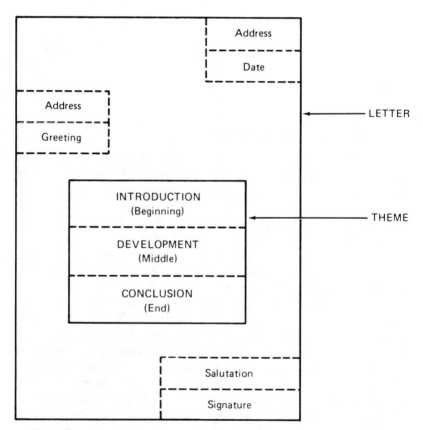

Figure 2

stood through time is the one that holds for the reader—and for the writer. As the writer, you can consider and explore only one idea at a time. The person reading your theme will progress one step at a time, moving from the first idea and its explanation to the second, and so on. It is only when the theme has been completely finished (written or read) that it creates the impression of a "whole" in the sense of blocks of paragraphs stacked on each other, and it does that only if you have built well. In order to build well, you must work one step at a time. And doing so makes the job of writing far easier.

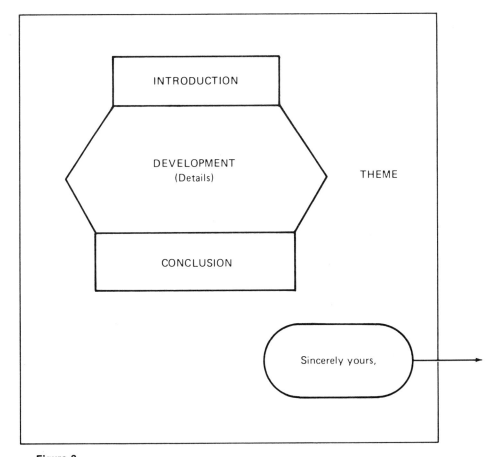

Figure 3

"THE THEME"

Paragraph 1
Paragraph 2
Paragraph 3
Paragraph 4
Paragraph 5

Figure 4

2. Developing Your Theme Clearly

The development, sometimes called the *middle* or the *body*, of the theme is the part that clearly and fully explains your thesis sentence idea to your reader. It provides the details and the order and the connections that your reader will need to understand your discussion and follow your argument. Because it comprises the majority of the things you have to say, the development is perhaps the most important part of your composition. And for many people it is also the most difficult part to write.

You are ready to begin working on the development of your theme as soon as you have a fairly firm idea of your thesis sentence, audience, and purpose. You start by looking again at your thesis sentence, trying

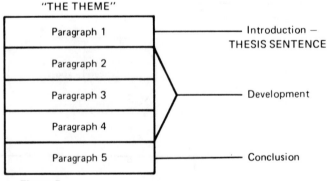

"THE THEME"

Figure 5

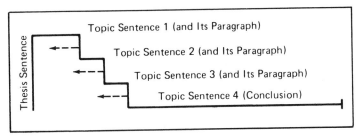

Figure 6

to determine what major ideas it contains as subcategories and what
kinds of supporting information will be required to explain and defend
it. Here is how a student used working papers to develop the "grapefruit craze" topic.

Working Papers—Theme Four

TENTATIVE THESIS: The big grapefruit craze of last year had a serious effect on the health of some of those people caught up in it.

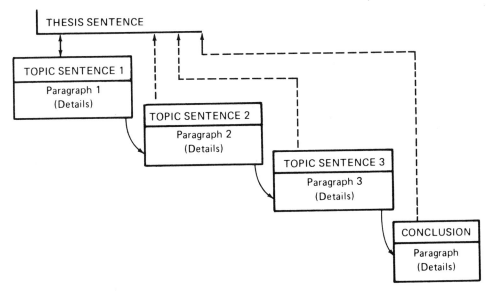

Figure 7

IDEAS:

1. Many people want to lose excess weight.
2. This fad diet promised to help them do so.
3. The idea was to eat grapefruit and only grapefruit each time you were hungry.
4. Several of my friends stayed on this diet for ten weeks.
5. While they lost weight in the process, the doctor explained that the diet was not good for them.
6. It took a month or more for most of them to get back to normal.

AUDIENCE: Instructor (or average adult).

PURPOSE: Use humor to demonstrate the potentially serious consequences of fad diets.

The initial framework here consists of the main ideas that the student planned to use to demonstrate the truth of the thesis sentence to the intended audience. Presumably, the student planned to use the details of the paragraphs to achieve the stated purpose.

How long the theme would be—how many paragraphs and how many words—would depend on the nature of the details the student had in mind and, of course, on the length assigned for the theme. The student is free to write a paragraph or two, or even three or four, about the human desire to lose weight. One paragraph might deal with statistics: how many Americans are overweight, how many say they are on diets, and so on. A paragraph or several might be devoted to overweight friends and relatives and how they got that way. And space might be devoted to the student's own battle with excess pounds. Thus, the first topic sentence idea ("Many people want to lose excess weight") might control one paragraph or many. Similarly, the explanation of the fad diet and the friends involved, the doctor's explanation, and the friends' recovery might take any number of paragraphs. Here is what the student whose working papers we have just seen eventually wrote.

Theme Four: Working Rough Draft

The big grapefruit craze of last year had a serious effect on the health of four of my friends. Like most of us, they wanted to shed excess pounds. According to HEW, over X percent of the American people can be classified as seriously overweight, and almost 100 percent of us have been "on diets" at one time or another. I would have been tempted by this diet myself, but I hate grapefruit.

The rules of the diet were simple. You could eat as much as you wanted, any time you wanted, but it was *only* grapefruit that you could eat. I am sure the founders of this absurdity meant it as a joke (or as a marketing device for grapefruit). In any case, in my considered opinion, a person of even average sanity would not accept such a torture, even under threat of death at the hand of an enemy, for more than a few days—a week at most. But Jeanne did it because she had dreams of being an actress; Marsha did it because she does whatever Jeanne does; Eileen did it to fit into a "size 7" dress; and Don did it because the other three dared him to. Masculine honor would permit nothing else. And all of them did it for ten—count them, *ten*—weeks.

The doctor explained as he attempted to put the pieces of their by now acidic stomachs back in place that it was not a good idea to follow fad diets for such a long time. He said that this particular diet [NOTE: check exactly what was said] . . . A day or two of almost any diet won't hurt, but ten weeks was just a little too much.

The upshot of the experience was that Eileen does fit into a size 7; Jeanne still wants to be an actress; and Marsha still does whatever Jeanne does. All of them looked better before they lost the weight. And Don—well, he upheld masculine honor with the girls, but now must struggle with the "99 pound weakling" complex. *He* does not look good in a size 7.

As you are planning out the paragraphs for your theme's development, it will help you to use what might be called the "test of because" as you formulate your topic sentences.

THESIS: Buses are not the solution to this city's transportation problems.

1. (Buses are not the solution to this city's transportation problems BECAUSE)
   Not all people will ride buses.

2. (Buses are not the solution to this city's transportation problems BECAUSE)
   Buses create problems as well as solving them.

3. (Buses are not the solution to this city's transportation problems BECAUSE)
   Other solutions to the problem would be better.

You do not have to write out your thesis sentence and the word *because* each time you list a reason; but that, in effect, is the process you are following to develop your topic sentences.

A student using this topic sentence list would plan to write a theme with one or more paragraphs devoted to each of the topic sentences on the list. Each paragraph would contain the details needed to explain the topic sentence idea and bring the theme to life for the reader. (See Figure 8.)

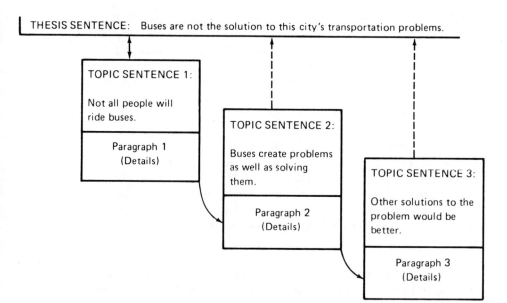

THESIS SENTENCE: Buses are not the solution to this city's transportation problems.

TOPIC SENTENCE 1:

Not all people will ride buses.

Paragraph 1
(Details)

TOPIC SENTENCE 2:

Buses create problems as well as solving them.

Paragraph 2
(Details)

TOPIC SENTENCE 3:

Other solutions to the problem would be better.

Paragraph 3
(Details)

Figure 8

You *develop* your theme—that is, you decide which ideas will be treated in your paragraphs—by subdividing these topic sentence ideas using the same process you applied when you worked with your topic in the first place. You could subdivide some of your topic sentence ideas or all of them.

TOPIC SENTENCE: Not all people will ride buses.
1. (Not all people will ride buses BECAUSE)
   Some people live too far from bus stops.
2. (Not all people will ride buses BECAUSE)
   Schedules make riding buses inconvenient for some people.

3. (Not all people will ride buses BECAUSE)
   Some people prefer the privacy and convenience of an automobile.

TOPIC SENTENCE: Buses create problems as well as solving them.
   1. (Buses create problems as well as solving them BECAUSE)
      Buses compete with cars for highway and parking space.
   2. (Buses create problems as well as solving them BECAUSE)
      Buses contribute to pollution.
   3. (Buses create problems as well as solving them BECAUSE)
      They guzzle fuel.

TOPIC SENTENCE: Other solutions to the problem would be better.
   1. (Other solutions to the problem would be better BECAUSE)
      Mandatory standards for size and efficiency for private automobiles
      would give people a transportation system they would use.
   2. (Other solutions to the problem would be better BECAUSE)
      Subways are quicker in the downtown area.

If necessary, you could subdivide each of your new subtopic ideas to develop the kind of depth and detail that are appropriate for longer compositions. *And* you can use this method of development to help you evaluate your thesis sentence and control the length of your final theme.

For example, you might decide that that the three topic sentences on your original list would make the theme too long. (See Figure 9.) If so, you can simply eliminate one of the original topic sentence ideas or treat fewer subtopics. If, on the other hand, the theme seems too short, you can add another topic sentence, add more subtopics, or provide more details in each paragraph as you write it. For example, paragraph 5 in Figure 9 might be developed in several ways:

A

Buses, moreover, create problems as well as solving them. It is certainly true that buses compete with cars for highway and parking space. If you've ever been stuck behind a row of buses going nowhere slowly, you know that is true.

B

Buses, moreover, create problems as well as solving them. If you travel at all during rush hour, you know that it is certainly true that buses compete

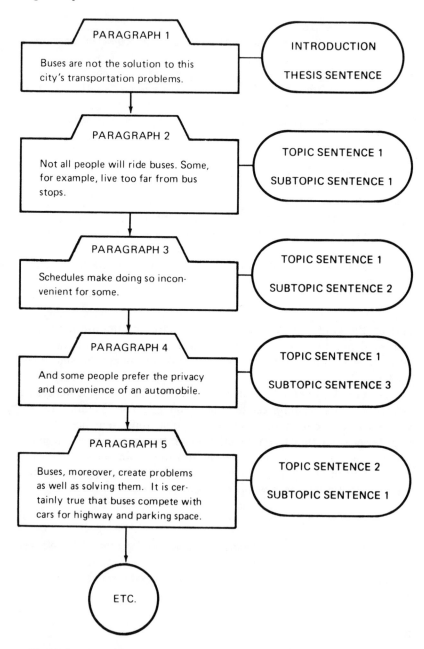

Figure 9

with cars for highway space. This morning, for example, I was stuck in rush hour traffic behind a broken-down bus for twenty minutes. On a day-to-day basis, I figure that bus traffic adds at least ten minutes to my forty-minute trip—because buses stop to take on and let off passengers and because they travel slowly. Sometimes they travel so slowly that they seem to be parked on the road, a motionless necklace of outdated beads strangling the neck of the city. The U.S. Department of Transportation estimates that in fact X percent of this country's buses are so old that they should no longer be used. The statistics on school buses are especially frightening in this regard, with Y percent considered downright dangerous.

It is the process of subdivision that keeps you from getting into a situation in which, after a few quick ideas, you have nothing more to say:

Buses are not the solution to this city's transportation problems. All people will not ride buses. Everyone knows that. And buses create problems such as pollution as well as solving them. Finally, other solutions to the problem would be better, as we all well know.

Thus, the motto of a theme writer might well be to *subdivide and conquer.*

Once you've generated your list of topic sentence and subtopic sentence ideas, you are well into the process of developing your theme. But you still have several more steps to take *before* you will be ready to write your paragraphs.

First, this is an appropriate time to step back and reevaluate your progress to date. Is your topic limited and specific enough so that you will be able to discuss it fully in the number of words you plan to write? Is your thesis sentence satisfying? Do your topic and subtopic sentence ideas support it, or is revision necessary somewhere? Your topic sentence ideas form your means for making these evaluations, and subdivision is your process.

Suppose, for example, that you have been asked to write a 500- to 750-word composition about your career choice. You have developed your list of ideas, worked up a tentative thesis sentence, and used subdivision to generate your topic and subtopic sentence concepts. Now, is your topic small enough?

TOPIC: My career choice

TENTATIVE THESIS: I chose to go into marketing as a career.

IDEAS: What I did to prepare in past. College for studying. Did well in school. Like challenges. Plans for future. Why I selected it. Business experience. Enjoy good money. Family business.

AUDIENCE ANALYSIS: Average adult.

PURPOSE: Explain why I chose this career, what I am doing to prepare for it, and what I hope to get out of it.

NOTE: Purpose seems to give me three major areas to explore as topic sentence possibilities:

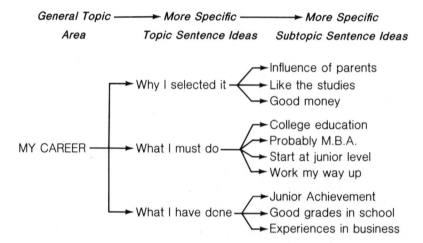

Whether your topic needs to be limited or not would depend on how much worthwhile information you as the writer had to provide to the reader. You might actually write a good 500-word theme about how your parents' influence convinced you to go into business or about your experiences in business or about your intent to work your way up. If you did not have enough pertinent information about any of these sub-topics, of course, your choice would be simple. Yet even if you had enough to say, you might well decide to stay with the larger topic.

As in so much of writing, the decision here is a matter of your judgment and sense of priority. Will the experience be more exciting, more intriguing for your reader if you deal with the smaller topic? Or will the larger one provide a greater sense of fulfillment? What was the intent of the original assignment? Which choice most closely fulfills that intent?

Let's assume in this case that you decide to remain with the original topic for now and to use the topic and subtopic sentence ideas you generated through the process of subdivision. The structure of your theme now looks like this:

A

I chose to go into marketing as a career.	**Thesis**
I selected this career for several reasons.	**Topic 1**
My parents influenced me greatly.	**Subtopic 1a**
I like the studies.	**Subtopic 1b**
There is good money in my future.	**Subtopic 1c**
I know what I must do to get there.	**Topic 2**
First I must get a college education.	**Subtopic 2a**
I will probably need an M.B.A.	**Subtopic 2b**
I will have to start at a junior level.	**Subtopic 2c**
I intend to work my way up.	**Subtopic 2d**
I have already done some things to get ready.	**Topic 3**
I belonged to Junior Achievement.	**Subtopic 3a**
I got good grades in school.	**Subtopic 3b**
I've had some experience in business.	**Subtopic 3c**

All you had to do to get from your list of ideas to this point was to subdivide and then take your subdivided phrases and make sentences out of them, once you had subordinated the lesser ideas. But you still have work to do before you are ready to write your paragraphs.

As a writer, it is your job to focus the experience of your paper for yourself and your reader—to select *the* central element of what you are to say, to express it in your thesis sentence, and to hold it in your mind's eye during the entire writing process. There are many, many possibilities from which to select.

B

TENTATIVE THESIS: Although other things contributed to my choice, it was my parents' influence that convinced me to select marketing as a career.

C

TENTATIVE THESIS: When my first Junior Achievement project finally succeeded, I knew I was hooked on marketing as a career.

D

TENTATIVE THESIS: I knew what I wanted out of life—a challenge, a future, some money—and I found it by accident in the library one day when I was looking for a career choice.

You can see how the new thesis sentences would control the development of the themes, and how each would be focused on some specific aspect of the experience though quite capable of dealing with all of it. It is just that other elements of the experience would be subordinated—that is, they would be made less important than the thesis sentence concept. The focus on the major aspect of the experience and the subordination of lesser ideas help make the theme as a whole into a satisfying unit for the reader.

You can develop these new thesis sentences using many of the same ideas you generated for your initial tentative thesis:

Although other things contributed to my choice, it was my parents' influence that convinced me to select marketing as a career.
1. I had always gotten good grades in school, especially in marketing-related courses.
2. I belonged to Junior Achievement and did well on the projects.
3. I like money and the other things possible in the future, such as a challenging work environment.
4. *But it was my parents most of all who influenced my career choice.*
5. The influence began when I was a small child and spent time with one or the other of my parents at their company during the day.
6. It continued when I was in grade school and was given marketing work to do (or so I believed) and was even paid for it.
7. And it continues now, when I plan to take over the family business someday, but only after having proved myself in the outside world.

If you were using this development pattern, you would plan to deal with the subordinated elements (the other things that contributed to your career decision) first. Each topic sentence might carry a paragraph or so of explanation, or all the topic sentences might be woven together into a single paragraph—depending on how important they are to an overall understanding of the idea being expressed. They too could be related to the main idea (e.g., "I always got good grades in school *because* I was motivated by my career ambition"), which would help hold the theme together. This section might be written last, as introductions should be, so that you would know how much space is to be allotted to it. Or, in this specific case, it might help get you started on the writing process; if so, write it first. Most of the rules about writing are breakable. What works for you is what counts.

Topic sentences 4–7 carry the weight of the theme's development. Topic sentence 4 ("My parents most influenced my career choice") brings the writer and the reader back to the main idea of the thesis (an important tool if you will be beginning with subordinated material as introduction). Topic sentences 5–7 ("The influence began; it continued; it continues now") take the reader chronologically through the writer's experience. Chronological order is a writing sequence that most readers follow easily and most writers find easy to use. You simply begin at the beginning of a story or chain of events and progress in time order through the story. Of course, you do not have to use chronological order. It is not always appropriate, and even if it is, there are other ways to develop your information. You will have a chance to practice many of these as you work with the material in the next chapter. For now, however, it is enough that you pay attention to the ordering pattern you select for your theme: Does it make sense in terms of the material and audience? Can you think of a better way? What would happen if you rearranged your information? Experimenting with your ordering patterns will help you grow as a writer. Analyzing your theme's developmental structures will help you determine whether your material is relevant to your topic and your thesis sentence or whether revision is required somewhere. And focusing your presentation will help make each theme as full and rich and satisfying as you can possibly make it at this stage of your writing career.

EXERCISE 1
Select tentative thesis sentence C or D and develop the topic and subtopic sentences you would need to write a 500- to 750-word theme. Of course, you will be inventing the information you need for the theme.

Once you have developed a structure that focuses on the main concept, provides enough relevant details to bring your theme to life, and presents them in an order that makes sense, write a working rough draft of the theme. Submit your rough draft and working papers to your instructor for comments, and then revise as appropriate to polish what you have done.

TENTATIVE THESIS: When my first Junior Achievement project finally succeeded, I know I was hooked on marketing as a career.

TENTATIVE THESIS: I knew what I wanted out of life—a challenge, a future, some money—and I found it by accident in the library one day when I was looking for a career choice.

EXERCISE 2

Select a topic for a 400- to 700-word theme. Prepare working papers that indicate your tentative thesis sentence, purpose, and audience analysis as well as your list of ideas. Then put your work aside for several days.

When you come back to it, rethink what you have done. Focus your thesis sentence so that it encompasses the heart of your theme idea. Subordinate lesser material if appropriate as part of your developmental work. Prepare two or three effective structures for your theme.

Submit what you have done to your instructor for comments. Then, comments in hand, prepare an effective composition for review.

EXERCISE 3

Examine the following student theme development patterns to see whether they follow a sensible order, whether the topic sentences relate to the thesis, and so on. Determine whether there is enough information in the topic sentences so that the writer will be able to develop a full and convincing presentation. Be prepared to defend your conclusions in class.

A

THESIS: *Fall is the best season of the year for me.*

TOPIC: It doesn't have the disadvantages of the other seasons.

TOPIC: I enjoy fall activities most of all.

TOPIC: I like shopping for winter clothes.

TOPIC: I even enjoyed being stranded in last fall's surprise blizzard.

B

THESIS: *In a childless marriage divorce should be a simple, inexpensive process.*

TOPIC: Children are what tie people together "for better or for worse."

TOPIC: Two adults who have entered a contract should be able to end it by mutual agreement.

TOPIC: My aunt and uncle spent thousands of dollars on their divorce.

TOPIC: No one benefits from complex divorce laws except lawyers.

C

THESIS: *The government does not have the right to protect citizens against themselves.*

TOPIC: As long as what I am doing does not hurt anyone else, the government should not stop me in order to "protect me."

TOPIC: Mandatory seat belt or air bags in cars violate a citizen's right to choose.

TOPIC: Cigarettes should be allowed (for adults) as long as proper warning labels are on the packages.

TOPIC: Alcohol, marijuana, and other "drugs" should similarly be legal.

TOPIC: It is only when citizens violate the rights of others (driving while intoxicated, for example) that the government has the right to interfere with their activities.

D

THESIS: Martell's essay is clear, coherent, and readable.

TOPIC: All the details make sense in context.

TOPIC: The argument flows easily and smoothly.

TOPIC: Many of the points are enlightening.

3. Beginning Your Theme Well

How you begin your theme depends on whether you are working on the rough draft or the polishing stages, on the topic you are dealing with, on the audience you want to reach, on the level of your skill, and on the amount of time you have to spend on the writing process. You already know that your rough draft should begin with your thesis sentence to get you started on the development of your ideas without getting sidetracked into what may turn out to be information you will discard later. For many short discussions, the thesis sentence coupled with one or two explanatory sentences form a sufficient beginning. It is with longer themes, 750 words and up, that the beginning becomes an "introduction" of a paragraph or more, requiring some special work and special skills. (See Figure 10.)

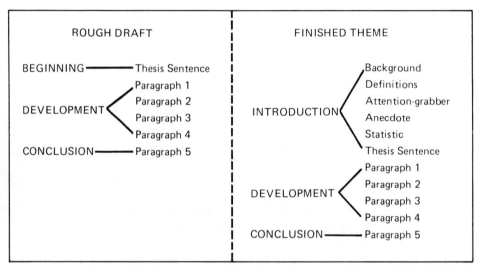

Figure 10

Like the beginning of a letter, the beginning of a theme provides the background information (history of the issue, definitions, and so on) that your reader may need to understand what you are talking about. Very often the introduction of a theme acts as an "attention grabber," using an unusual fact or intriguing anecdote to draw the reader into the main idea. A composition will sometimes begin by stating in a general way the issue that the writer wishes to focus on in particular during the course of the theme. And you know the beginning of the theme usually states the thesis sentence.

Of course, not all theme introductions will perform all of these functions. If, for example, the topic is a simple one, the reader will not need background information or definitions. An amusing anecdote would be out of place in a serious theme. And some compositions do not even begin with a statement of the thesis (or ever make one directly, for that matter), though it is wise for you to include one in your initial themes. You will find that some introductions are longer than others, depending again on the nature of the topic, the needs of the reader, and the length of the paper itself. As part of your planning, you will need to allot sufficient space for introductory material so that your reader will be ready to understand what you have written. Your temptation initially will be to allow for too much introduction: A paragraph is sufficient for a 600- to 700-word theme. If you have more than two paragraphs of introduction in a theme of that length, you should probably reconsider your apportionment of space.

In many ways introducing a theme is like introducing a person. Before you would attempt to introduce someone to a group, you would get some facts: name, hobbies, family, job—whatever is relevant to the specific situation at hand. The same is true of the theme: Before you *can* introduce it, you must perform the prewriting tasks you learned earlier, and you should have a good idea of how your theme will develop. Many students think that they "can't write" because they sit down to write an introduction and find themselves with a "mental block" and nothing to say. Introductions are *not* written first. Begin your rough draft with your thesis sentence, and come back to write your introduction later. Here is what happened when one student began by trying to write the introduction rather than taking the prewriting steps we have learned:

The Mark Hike—Draft

The day started out simply enough with a bugle call (off key) interrupting the chirping of the birds and the chatter of the younger girls who were already awake even though it was just becoming light outside. It was to be the "big mark hike day" today, and the girls who had never been on one were excited. This day had been a tradition in our troop since our mothers' mothers had been girls.

To explain it simply, the big mark hike was the day when each girl would go alone into the woods, demonstrating what she had learned about safety and hiking and survival by marking her trail and following it back out. There were no other rules, really, except that no one was to do anything that she knew was dangerous, and that each girl would be tested against the best she could do. It was you and yourself.

This was not my first mark hike—I had done it the year before, and so I was not taking the whole thing as seriously as some of the others. I knew—or thought I knew—what they would experience. The solitude, frightening at first, but then reassuring. The temptation not to go too far, and the judgment of how far was far enough. The sense of relief when it was over and the sense of accomplishment that you had done it. So I was not taking it too seriously. And I didn't bother to pack all the things I should have taken. After all, these were *my* woods. But even so, there was no excuse for not having that compass along.

Of course, the obvious thing happened and I got lost. I was upset for a while, but got my bearings again soon. Everything turned out all right since I got out of the woods safely. I will remember to be more careful next time.

From beginning to end, the entire theme seems to function to undercut the value of the "mark hike" experience to the writer. The writer begins with chirping birds and chattering younger girls, moves through an explanation of what the mark hike is, and goes on to the statement that she herself is not taking the whole thing seriously. Even in the concluding paragraph the writer undercuts the value of the experience still further ("I was upset for a while . . . Everything turned out all right since I got out of the woods safely"). If you were analyzing this theme, you would rightly conclude that the topic seemed to have little importance to the writer, and you would probably wonder why she chose it at all.

What is missing from the theme is the careful consideration that is part of the prewriting process. The writer still needs to determine the relevance of the topic to herself and to the reader, and to focus on it clearly. She still must subordinate the evidence and formulate a thesis sentence that will hold the story together and give it meaning. It was just too tempting for her, apparently, to "tell the story and get it over with." In so doing, however, she lost the impact that she might have made. Working papers would have been an appropriate aid.

Working Papers: Mark Hike

PURPOSE: To explain how the mark hike helped me to understand myself much better.

AUDIENCE: Average adult

THESIS: The most important single day in my life occurred in the middle of the summer when I was fourteen at a girl scout camp in upper New York State.

IDEAS:

1. What the mark hike is.
2. History of the mark hike.
3. Story of what happened.
   a. How the day started.
   b. What happened in the woods.
   c. How I felt.
   d. *Why it was important to me.*

PLAN: Begin with thesis sentence; conclude with importance of experience.

Once the student had gone back to do the working papers, she was ready to rewrite the theme. As you read the new theme, notice how much stronger the entire story has become because of the focusing that the student did. As you read, see if you can determine how the structure of the theme works to convey the writer's ideas.

The Most Important Day—Draft 2

The most important single day in my life occurred in the middle of the summer when I was fourteen at a girl scout camp in upper New York State.

Thesis

The day started out simply enough with a bugle call (off key) interrupting the chirping of the birds and the chatter of the younger girls who were already awake even though it was just becoming light outside. It was to be the "big mark hike day" today, and the girls who had never been on one were excited. This day had been a tradition in our troop since our mothers' mothers had been girls.

1

To explain it simply, the big mark hike was the day when each girl would go alone into the woods, demonstrating what she had learned about safety and hiking and survival by marking her trail and following it back out. There were no other rules, really, except that no one was to do anything she knew was dangerous, and that each girl would be tested against the best she could do. It was you and yourself.

2

3   This was not my first mark hike—I had done it the year before, and so I was not taking the whole thing as seriously as some of the others. I knew—or thought I knew—what they would experience. The solitude, frightening at first, but then reassuring. The temptation not to go too far, and the judgment of how far was far enough. The sense of relief when it was over and the sense of accomplishment that you had done it. So I was not taking it too seriously. And I didn't bother to pack all the things I should have taken. After all, these were *my* woods. But even so, there was no excuse for not having that compass along.

4   Of course, the obvious thing happened. We all set out in high hopes and great expectations, and I got lost.

5   Something distracted me. I'm not quite sure what it was—the beauty of the day, sharp and clear, the woods, a fawn. I just don't know. But somehow I stopped paying attention, stopped marking my trail, and lost my bearings. And panicked. My heart started beating fast, I began to sweat, and I *knew* I was lost, perhaps for good. And not only that, I hadn't been careful and would be *humiliated* in front of the others if they ever did find me. What was I to do?

6   If you have never been fourteen and lost in the woods, you might not understand that this was *the* most catastrophic event in the history of the world, and that I was at its center. And then something happened to me. I don't know if you would call it "growing up" or "finding yourself" or just what. But I did both. I found something inside of me, something which was a center of myself, something which said, "*you* are in control of yourself, and *you* can handle it." Once I had that, the woods were indeed my woods.

Conclusion   I returned from my second mark hike after having only been gone an hour or so. I was the first one back, and never explained why. But what I learned that day has never deserted me and has extended the borders of my woods to wherever I go.

The basic structure of "The Most Important Day" now looks something like Figure 11. The thesis sentence sets an overall path, with the rest of the theme's structure functioning to amplify and explain that idea. All of the developmental paragraphs relate back to the thesis sentence, some more strongly than others. The first development paragraph introduces the day ("The day started out simply enough . . . ") and the idea of the mark hike. The second paragraph functions to explain the first ("The big mark hike was . . . "), while the third gives background for the important day. The fourth paragraph quickly and

INTRODUCTION:		Thesis Sentence
DEVELOPMENT:	Paragraph 1	Background . . .day starts
	Paragraph 2	Explanation . . .mark hike is
	Paragraph 3	Background . . .done it before
	Paragraph 4	Explanation . . .got lost
	Paragraph 5	Explanation . . .how I felt
	Paragraph 6	Explanation . . .what I found
CONCLUSION:		Generalizes Experience

Figure 11

simply explains what happened ("I got lost"). The fifth paragraph explains how the writer felt when she was lost.

It is the sixth and final developmental paragraph, however, that begins to make the point of the experience clear. Only now are we told why the mark hike is important to the writer ("I found something inside of me"). The concluding paragraph, finally, emphasizes what has come before by showing how it will be a reference point for the rest of the writer's life.

Once you have an effective thesis sentence and a good idea of what your theme will say, you are in a position to experiment with various introductory paragraphs to see which will be most effective for your topic and your intended audience. You will find that the way you introduce your theme will alter its tone and style and effect. You may want to change your thesis sentence and presentation slightly to encompass your new outlook on your material. As you read the four new introductory paragraphs that students wrote for the "most important day" theme, analyze their effectiveness. How would each change the theme as a whole? Which is most successful?

The Most Important Day—Introduction 1

The day started out simply enough with an off-key bugle call breaking the chirping of the birds and the chatter of the younger girls who had never been on a mark hike before. This was not my first mark hike, so I was not taking it as seriously as some of the others. *Little did I dream that this day in the middle of the summer of my fourteenth year would be the most important day in all my life.*   **Thesis**

The Most Important Day—Introduction 2

People "find themselves," to coin a phrase, in different ways and at different times. Perhaps we "find ourselves" again and again, I don't know. *But my first experience of myself occurred one scary early morning in the summer of my fourteenth year.*

Thesis

The Most Important Day—Introduction 3

For the girl scouts in troop 107, the big mark hike was a culmination of everything they had learned about camping and safety and hiking and survival. To explain it simply, the big mark hike was the day when each girl would match herself against the woods, going as far as she dared, doing as much as she could without violating any of the safety rules she had learned. *Since this was to be my second mark hike, I never guessed that it was also to be my most important single day.*

Thesis

The Most Important Day—Introduction 4

Something distracted me. I'm not quite sure what it was—the beauty of the day, sharp and clear, the woods, a fawn. I just don't know. *But somehow I stopped paying attention, stopped marking my trail, lost my bearings, and learned in the next few moments more about myself than I ever had before.*

Thesis

The first sample introduction functions as a "stage setter," introducing the day and the concept of the mark hike before moving into the thesis sentence. The second sample introduces the experience of "finding yourself," while the third begins by giving background information, telling the reader what the mark hike is so that he or she will be prepared to understand the experience to come. The fourth, finally, starts in the middle of the day to get the reader into the experience quickly.

As you begin to experiment with your own themes, you will find many ways of introducing them. Each will set a slightly different direction for the theme to follow. But it is best when working on your rough draft to begin with your thesis sentence. When you are fairly well satisfied with the content and structure of your theme, you will be ready to devise the most effective way of introducing it.

EXERCISE 1

Evaluate the following student themes in light of what you now know about structure, development, and introductions. Does the writer have a clearly focused thesis sentence? Does the theme subordinate the experience and the evidence to the overall concept expressed in the thesis? How might the themes be improved?

Be prepared to support your analyses in class and to suggest several possible thesis sentences for themes in which they are lacking or should be improved.

A

Energy Conservation

Turning off lights helps to conserve energy as does remembering to shut off television sets when you are not watching. Home insulation helps a lot, especially if you live in a climate which gets very hot in summer or very cold in winter.

Setting your air conditioner thermostat as high as is comfortable in summer will save energy, as will keeping your winter heat setting very low. Also effective is keeping the oven door closed when baking.

B

Apartment Dogs

I have three dogs myself and I live in an apartment, so I guess that I really should not complain about my neighbors. But the thing of it is, I have three very small dogs (miniature poodles) which are quiet (well, at least most of the time) and are kept under control. But some of my neighbors have *very large* dogs—German shepherds are most common, but there are several even larger, such as a great Dane, a St. Bernard, and an Afghan. And there are a couple of wire haired terriers, which are small dogs, but hysterical and in need of acres of room to unwind themselves.

Sometimes I can't determine whether it is more of a cruelty to the people who must share the apartment with those terrors or to the dogs themselves, being cooped up. But leaving that aside as none of my business, I do know that I am tired of doing bathroom chores for someone else's pet. I am tired of hearing the hounds of the Baskervilles outside my bedroom windows. And I am tired of being jumped on by the less-than-clean-pawed occupants of neighboring domiciles.

I am in full favor of people sharing their lives with dogs. I do it myself. But I think some common sense is in order. If people won't (or can't) find it for themselves, I think it needs to be applied to them by apartment managers or by city and county regulation.

D

Taxes

Taxes are too high for the majority of Americans. We pay an ungodly amount of their money in taxes. The services which the government provides in return are not worth the cost. Private companies could provide those same services for less money, and we could select only those services we wanted (such as schools for children) and not pay for those of no interest (such as welfare payments).

I also believe that taxes are out of control because people have lost the authority to say what is being done with their tax money. For example, I cannot specify that my taxes will go to pay for programs which I believe in, but must allow them to be put into a general fund that will pay for anything the government wants.

D

A Kilowatt at a Time

Saving evergy requires having a plan, not only on a national or state or local level, but as individuals and as families. The first thing we must do is to investigate a bit, to find out which appliances use the most energy, and how to use them efficiently. The next thing is to check your home's insulation (or your apartment's, if you can) to see if it meets local standards. If not, you would investigate the possibility of adding insulation. And of course, weatherstripping and other minor repairs cost very little and save a lot.

The next thing to do is to learn how to read your electric meter, if you don't already know how. Your utility company will give you the information (the same is true for your gas and water meters). Read your meter, and note the reading. Then take a conservation step like turning off your air conditioner for an hour. Read the meter again. Then read it after an hour with your air conditioner on. That will tell you how much energy it takes to keep your home cool for one hour.

Maybe you think it is worth it, and maybe you don't. But the point is that you will, *know* what each energy using device in your home takes. Then you can decide what you need and what you don't, and form a plan to conserve energy, one kilowatt at a time.

EXERCISE 2

Read the following student theme. Determine which sentence is the thesis sentence. Then write several introductory paragraphs using information provided in the theme itself (or inventing information where necessary). Which introduction do you think is most effective for the topic? Why?

An Alternate Life Style

My wife Sandy and I have been married for a year now, and we are still firm in our decision not to have any children.

It is surprising how this choice of an alternate life style upsets people, and not just the potential "grandparents" and aunts and uncles whose fondest hopes have been dashed by our lack of attendance to duty. No, many people seem to care that we won't be changing any diapers. Sandy gets it worse than I do, since in our culture, women are supposed to want to be mothers while fatherhood is somewhat (but not much) lower on the scale. But even when I tell perfectly sane people that I don't want any kids, they try to convince me that I do! "Don't you want a Jim Junior?" they say, or "You'll change your mind, give yourself time." As if it was a goal that I couldn't quite reach.

I don't know why people get that way, unless it is because what seems like a very rational choice to us is threatening to a decision which they can't change (because they already have the kids) or a decision which they have not got the courage to make in the first place—to have no kids. I do know that Sandy and I will have the financial freedom to live as we wish pretty much. And more than that, we will have the time to grow as people, to experience ourselves and each other without the burden of tending first to the needs of a helpless other person. Maybe we will miss something. In fact, I am sure that we will. But we believe that we will gain more than we will miss, and that this alternate life style will be a successful choice for us.

EXERCISE 3

One of the major functions of an introductory paragraph or paragraphs is getting the favorable attention of the reader (an introduction in bad taste may get attention, but not the kind you want). Some themes begin with an unusual fact or statistic, an interesting (but relevant) story or anecdote, or a pertinent quotation. Assume that you are writing a theme about divorce in America (you may subdivide that topic if you wish). Take the prewriting steps necessary to set up such a theme, and write a thesis sentence that focuses on your ideas. Then write an introductory paragraph using an unusual fact(s) or statistic(s), one using an anecdote or story, and one using a pertinent quotation. For the purposes of this assignment, you may invent your data, but it would be a good idea to familiarize yourself with the reference sources available to you in your library (speakers' handbooks, quotation handbooks, etc.) at your earliest convenience so that you may use them as the occasion arises.

4. Concluding Your Theme Effectively

Because it is the last part of your theme your reader sees and, thus, the part most likely to be remembered, the conclusion of your theme deserves your careful attention.

Sometimes, in your shorter themes, the conclusion will consist of just a sentence or two summarizing your main ideas or restating your thesis sentence in other words. This is a very satisfying kind of conclusion, linking your theme together as a unit like a necklace when you put it on and close it. (See Figure 12.)

This is not a very difficult conclusion for you to write, since it requires, essentially, an emphatic restatement of your thesis sentence, sometimes using new details, usually using a variant sentence structure or vocabulary choice so that the conclusion does not seem redundant. And since restatement is a short conclusion, it is an appropriate one for most of the themes you will be writing in your freshman composition course.

Other compositions, those of 750 words or more, may require a longer conclusion (in any theme most of the writing space should be devoted to the development of the ideas, with the introduction and conclusion carefully expressed, powerful, but relatively brief sections). Conclusions often serve to focus your reader's attention on your most convincing argument and use the most startling fact or most lively anecdote to do so. Other times, conclusions reach out, expanding the main idea of the theme into the larger world, showing its relevance to issues, to history, to the reader, and so on. Very often, conclusions do a

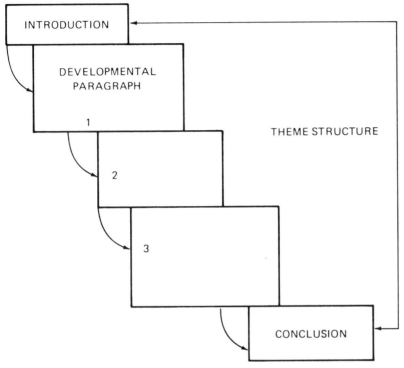

INTRODUCTION

DEVELOPMENTAL
PARAGRAPH

1

THEME STRUCTURE

2

3

CONCLUSION

Figure 12

little of each, as they do in the following student themes about competition for grades in college.

A

Competition for Grades My Freshman Year
(Conclusion: Planned to Summarize and Restate)

For me, the hardest part of my freshman year at college was knowing that the competition for grades would be so much keener than I was used to. I was not sure that I could succeed under these circumstances, and I found my uncertainty to be very stressful.

In the first place, I had come from a very small, rural high school. There were only about 50 people (47 to be exact) in my graduating class. Even though I was valedictorian, I was not sure that meant much when it came to the competition at the university.

Second, I was planning to be a doctor, which meant that I would be taking chemistry, biology, history, and freshman composition. All of the classes except history had the reputation of being "flunk out" classes—which meant that they "separated the men from the boys." And I wasn't even interested in history.

Finally, I knew that many of the people in those classes also wanted a medical degree and would be willing to work very hard for it—as hard as I had always been willing to work for what I wanted. It was not until after I discovered that I could compete successfully that the very stressful beginning of my freshman year yielded to enjoyment of a new and exciting place.

B

Dealing with Freshman Worries
(Conclusion: Planned for Most Convincing Argument)

The initial few months of a college freshman's life are made unnecessarily miserable by (a) the fact that the freshman probably has many false beliefs about college life, (b) the fact that college is a new and somewhat frightening experience for most people, and (c) the fact that this college and most others do little or nothing to help the freshman adjust.

Most college freshman students have looked foward for many years to their first day at the university. Their parents have "worked and scraped and planned and saved." Or their own career goals make college, and succeeding at college, an absolute necessity. Society in general seems to expect a post-high school age person to be in college. But even if you're here "just because," it is still important to succeed.

Most new students come to their first day on a college campus armed with some amazing misconceptions. Half the students flunk freshman English. Professor X means doom. You have to take four solids (when you really do not). It would be well for someone—including both college people and more senior students—to explain the ropes, to get students oriented before they start classes.

And the orientation should continue through the first months when the new student has to cope with the classes and the workload and perhaps the not so good grades. Especially if you are used to getting excellent grades, that first "C" can be very hard to take.

With a little help and guidance, a great number of the students at this university could have a more enjoyable and a more successful freshman year. That year could be the foundation for a better four years, indeed, for a better life. Rather than instilling or making permanent the fear of failure which the young person brings to the first days at a university, the school could be a teacher in the profoundest sense, instilling knowledge and confidence in new students lest they look elsewhere to find it.

C

Who Really Fails When a Student Fails?
(Planned Conclusion: Expansion to Include the Larger World)

It is perhaps a truism that things are most delicate in their beginnings. So too is a college education.

In a large number of ways, it is the first few months of the freshman year that "make or break" a student. In a new and somewhat frightening situation, perhaps on his or her own for the first time, the student is faced with stiffer competition than ever before, harder classes, and more work. At the same time, the novice student may have to adjust to sharing a room with an unfriendly stanger and making do with what dormitory cafeterias semi-seriously call "food."

This trek from teenage, dependent status to young adulthood is not an easy one. Now, more than ever, many students need a helping hand. They need someone to bother to say, "Take it easy on yourself, sometimes it takes a while." Or, "Everyone has a too hard class now and then; doesn't mean you're stupid." Or even, "It's hard to learn that stuff; forget it for now and I'll help you later."

Perhaps it seems naive and unrealistic to you that I would expect one person to help another in the fashion I just suggested. Well, make no mistakes. I *don't* expect it. But it saddens me that it is not present here. It was not the first time I was a freshman here seven years ago, and it still is not.

You see, I was one of the ones that the "flunk out" courses flunked out. I hope the professors are proud in their success. I was one of the ones who could not adjust or could not do it fast enough. It has taken me seven years to repair the damage to my psyche and to find the strength to try it again.

Maybe I am stronger for having gone this round. But it seems to me that the larger purpose of the university—the passing of the wisdom of the ages from one generation to the next—is ill served by the callous disregard for the "marginal"or "immature" student. It is true that human kindness cannot be legislated into place and professors cannot be forced to have compassion. Yet, if the university is interested in serving its society, compassion could be part of a professor's job, and his or her tenure could depend on how many students learned what there was to teach. It seems to me in this place at least that students are the primary society being served and at the same time the forgotten one.

If you've planned properly and developed your themes well, you will probably discover that your conclusions are the easiest part of your themes to write. Your major challenge will be in organizing your material so that you can build to a climax if that is suitable for your topic, so that you can end on a reasonably important part of the experience or with some expression of insight (as in the final version of the "mark hike" theme) or with the relevance of what you have just said to some larger issue of concern to the reader. A successful conclusion grows naturally out of the process of understanding and focusing the topic and developing it so that the center of the experience remains at the center of the theme. Whether you conclude by circling back to your beginning or by reaching out for the larger world, your conclusion itself is worthy of your careful attention because it is this part of your theme's structure that, like the final piece in a puzzle, locks what you have to say in place and makes it whole. A good composition with a weak conclusion may not get its message across because it never comes together. But a good theme with a strong conclusion is like a puzzle with its last piece fitting in exactly: If you stand back and consider, the parts seem to disappear into the harmony of the whole and the puzzle—or the theme—becomes a single working unit.

EXERCISE 1
Reread the student themes about competition for grades. In your judgment which is the most effective and why? Analyze the structure of each theme as you are deciding. Consider the introductions, developments, and conclusions. What has the writer's perspective on the topic and on life in general to do with your ultimate opinion of the theme? If you were grading these themes in competition with each other, what grade would you give each? Be prepared to discuss your reasoning in class.

EXERCISE 2
Select some aspect of the "competition for grades in college" topic for a 400- to 600-word theme. (You may select another topic with the approval of your instructor.) Prepare your working papers and develop your theme's structure, making sure to focus on the central part of the

topic in your thesis sentence and to subordinate lesser material. Then write your theme.

EXERCISE 3
Choose a theme that you've written for a previous assignment or select one of the sample student themes in Unit One. See what happens to the impact of the theme you selected when you rewrite the introduction and the conclusion, the first time to make each as poor and weak as possible, the second time to make each as strong and poignant as you can. What kinds of data and skills were required to write the good introduction and conclusion? What did you deliberately do wrong when you wrote the weak ones?

Submit your work and your analysis to your instructor. If you wish, you may use a table like Table 6 or a list for your analysis rather than writing out paragraphs.

TABLE 6

Revision Analysis Chart

	Strong Introduction	*Weak Introduction*	*Strong Conclusion*	*Weak Conclusion*
Kinds of details	1. 2. 3.			
Techniques	1. 2.			
Avoided				
Relation to theme				
Etc.				

unit Two
the finished theme

chapter 5

holding your theme together

1. The Process of Revision

By the time you begin to "revise" your theme, you will have already accomplished a number of very important writing jobs. You will have understood and explored your topic and developed a thesis sentence that focuses on your main discussion path. You will have developed topic sentences as your main supporting points and built paragraphs around them. You will have gathered and evaluated many ideas and facts, using some and eliminating others. And in doing all of this you may have started and stopped, written and rewritten your theme several times. But finally you were satisfied that you had an acceptable rough draft, that you had the main ideas necessary to support a definitive thesis sentence, that the order in which you expressed them made sense, and that you had considered the need of the reader to understand as well as your own need to express your ideas and get on to something else.

You are now ready to consider revision. This means taking a sharper look at the audience you want to reach, at your material and your ways of expressing it, and at the style of what you write. Some of what you will be reading in this unit will be familiar to you from Unit One and perhaps from earlier studies of composition; thus, your study now may be in part a review. But both *re-vision* and *re-view* mean "to look and see again." This second chance to deal with these aspects of the writing process will allow you to consider relationships between them that may not have been apparent as you struggled to learn about each.

For example, now that you understand the basics of structuring an effective theme, you are ready to spend some time experimenting with the various patterns of organization that writers commonly use to develop and present ideas. You are ready to see which pattern is most convincing for *your* material and *your* audience, rather than simply accepting the first one that comes to mind. And now that you have had some experience writing the paragraphs that constitute a rough draft, you are ready to practice and incorporate a great variety of paragraph types into your writing. Your sentences and your very diction will come under scrutiny as part of the work of this unit. Your goal will be to take that acceptable rough draft and transform it into the most elegant, most expressive piece of writing of which you are capable. You still are not looking for something fancy or "high-falutin' " as your finished theme, but you will be concentrating your attention on the finer points of what you have to say. Here, for example, is how one student handled the revision of an acceptable rough draft by focusing on adding connective words, filling out paragraphs so that they were substantive blocks of communication, and clarifying sentence structure and details so that the theme made the best impression that he could create in the week he had to do the assignment:

On My Honor (Acceptable Rough Draft)

This college puts me "on my honor" not to cheat on exams and papers. I am going to use this theme to explore what being "on my honor" means to me and to others in this school with the hope of generating a better understanding of what is actually going on in many students' lives.

In the traditional and well-understood sense, being "on your honor" means that you give your word that you will not cheat. No one keeps watch over you in exams, and the professor is to assume that you have done your papers without help from anyone and without copying any reference sources. That is what it is supposed to mean to "be on your honor."

The problem with "being on your honor" is that it no longer works in

American society if it ever did. With the crush of people competing for everything, from grades to jobs, most students can't afford to be on their honor, especially if they can't be sure that other people are. As with all examples of honesty, the person who is honest in this situation is at a disadvantage when compared with the person who is not, especially if no one is checking.

It is for this reason that I am suggesting that this college reevaluate its honor policy. If tests were monitored and if professors made some effort to insure that students themselves wrote their themes and did their other homework honestly and without help, those students who would be honest in any case could afford to be "on their honor," and those students who would violate the honor system in any case might be dissuaded from so doing. The ultimate effect would be a more honest, more honorable, and more realistic situation for students functioning in a competitive world.

This is an acceptable rough draft because the student has focused his attention on one specific, worthwhile topic and has developed it clearly and completely. A reader would understand the student's point of view and would be able to evaluate it on the basis of the evidence provided by the theme itself. Everything in the theme is relevant to the topic—there is no extraneous material.

However, the student has yet to focus on providing the kinds of rich detail that bring excitement and color to what is being said. Each paragraph could be further developed, and the initial paragraph includes a purpose statement ("I am going to use this theme to explore what being 'on my honor' means to me . . ."), which usually is not a good idea. The purpose of the theme should be clear from the thesis statement itself. Revision will allow this student to concentrate on these matters and try out various patterns for organizing and presenting ideas.

On My Honor (Revision 1)

I have written this theme "on my honor," and it may cost me dearly to have done so.

In the traditional and well-understood sense, being "on your honor" means that you give your word that you will not cheat. If you are writing a theme, you will *not* take one from the fraternity files and you will *not* get help from your sister who teaches English composition at Harvard and you will *not* copy it from a reference book which your roommate checked out of the library some years ago and forgot to return. If you are taking an examination and you are "on your honor," you will *not* have sneaked a copy of the questions out of your instructor's office, and you will *not* have written the answers on your wrists or other anatomical parts, and, finally, you will *not* be copying from the ugly looking girl across the aisle from you just because she gets good grades. You, my friend, are *on your honor.*

The problem with being on your honor is that it no longer works in American society, if it ever did. With the crush of people competing for everything from grades to jobs, most students find the honor system to be a luxury they cannot afford. It is hard enough even if you are a good student to get decent grades so that you have a shot at a decent job without competing with someone's Harvard-employed sister or a musty reference book or a long-eyed cheater. And so, in order to protect the honest students, those who take being on their honor seriously, colleges ought to make an effort to monitor tests and to insure that students do their own homework and write their own themes. It is time that this college entered the real world of the late twentieth century, a world in which people cheat on their income taxes and steal from their employers and roll through stop signs in spite of the penalties, to protect those honest students by doing away with the honor system, or at the very least, by spot checking to make sure that it works as well as possible. The ultimate effect of such an effort by the college would be to insure a more honest, more honorable and more realistic situation for students functioning in today's competitive world.

And since I have written this theme "on my honor," I cannot help but wonder how it will compare with the themes written by my classmates who were also on their honor and of course took it as seriously as I did. Or did they? That, ultimately, is the question.

The first revision of "On My Honor" focuses on the topic more carefully than the rough draft did, clarifying the impact of the topic and thesis on the writer and the reader. More details, and more specific details, have been provided to bring the theme to life. While work yet remains to smooth out the presentation, the new theme provides a fuller and more satisfying treatment than the old one did.

Several revisions, in fact, might be necessary before the student would feel that his theme constituted his best effort. Like the rough-draft procedures, the revision process requires willingness to experiment with what you have to say, to try something and throw it out and then try something else. In some senses, too, the separation of revision from rough-draft procedures is an artificial one. Studying in this fashion has allowed you to focus first on the major steps in building an effective theme without being sidetracked by alternate ways of doing things and without splitting your attention between the building of a structure and its refinement.

What you learn about revision in this unit will become a part of how you approach a writing assignment. You will always know about unity and coherence. You will be aware of the organizational patterns available to you, and you will have developed skill in writing various kinds of paragraphs. What you learn about sentences and diction will enter into your rough drafts as well. Never again will writing and revising be entirely separate for you.

Your goal now, as you begin this second unit of the book, is to make each theme as perfect as you can. That may entail writing a rough draft and then revising it—many people use just this procedure to avoid having polished paragraphs that will be discarded later. Or you may prefer to build your structure of topic sentences and then write your paragraphs, polishing as you go. Or some other approach may work best for you.

Whatever works best for you is the correct way to write. And what you learn about revision now will help you make your writing dynamic and give impact to what you have to say—very useful skills to have both in the classroom and in "real-world" writing situations.

EXERCISE 1
Read and evaluate the following student themes. What might be done to improve them as rough drafts? In other words, have the students provided clear, full discussions of worthwhile thesis sentences? Be prepared to defend your conclusions in class.

A

On the Road

You asked what I like to do for fun, well it's foot loose and fancy free for me. I like getting my stuff together (and not much stuff, either) and heading out somewhere. Anywhere will do.

I like the unstructured feeling of being on the road. Hitchhiking will do if no wheels are available, just going anywhere and taking any turn in the road to see what appears on the other side. It's not very elegant and this is probably not such a good theme in any case, but that's the way I am.

B

On the Road

When I think of being "on the road," I think of the year I spent back-packing through Europe. I went to France and Rome and Germany and Switzerland and Austria. I even went to Egypt.

Being on the road that year was just about the very best thing that ever happened to me. It was a fantastic vacation and I saw all the sights. It taught me independence and self-sufficiency, lessons which will be valuable to me for all my life.

C

On the Road

Being "on the road" has to mean but one thing to an American in the twentieth century. Sure, some of us travel for fun, spending miles and miles tootling through countries. Others enjoy a drive in the country on weekends. But that's not it. Being "on the road" in America has to mean fighting the traffic to get where you are going, being stuck in a miles long parking lot which should have been a roadway, sitting in overheating cars with overheating tempers—in short, part of the American way of life.

Being on the road in this fashion is good for you. It builds patience and perseverance as you sit calmly waiting for a light to change and for the person in the car ahead to notice. Of course, you would not honk your horn, since so doing would disrupt the serenity of the city air. And being on the road builds your ability to get along with people. The maniac on your rear fender becomes but one of God's creatures. The guy who just cut you off obviously has something more important on his mind. And the traffic cop who only enforces laws in your case teaches you to attend to business and not be distracted.

But most of all, being on the road teaches you to manipulate mechanical objects such as wrenches and jacks and nuts and bolts and butterfly valves and so on to keep the car operating long after it should have died. Not everyone can perform miracles in this fashion, and if you can, you are lucky.

Because of these benefits to being on the road, I suggest that we adopt a system where everyone has to be at work at the same time and everyone leaves at the same time, where highway departments build roads using last year's traffic patterns rather than next year's, and where road construction can only be done during rush hour. This certainly would enhance the effect of being on the road and improve the American character beyond belief.

EXERCISE 2
Select a theme that you have written for a previous class assignment or one from this book (with your instructor's consent). Evaluate it: Is it an acceptable rough draft? What needs to be done to enhance its structure? Then look at it in terms of the finer points. Could it be expressed more clearly? Are the connections between ideas present or is the reader guessing? Could there be more variety in the paragraphs and sentences? Are precise words used to express the writer's meanings?

Revise the theme as necessary to make it as elegant as you can. You may have to return to the rough-draft procedures before revising makes any sense.

2. Patterns of Organization

For many of your college writing assignments, you will be asked to handle new and difficult concepts, to think carefully and fully about ideas, and to organize facts and evidence to support your major arguments. In "real-life" writing circumstances, the writing pattern will not always grow naturally out of what you have to say. And there will often be several patterns operating in the same theme: an overall pattern and a series of smaller patterns governing paragraphs or parts of paragraphs.

If you haven't selected an effective overall pattern as part of your rough-draft writing procedure, revising will give you an opportunity to do so. And if you have already selected a pattern for your theme, revising will give you a chance to reconsider: Perhaps another overall pattern would be more effective. And revising is also the time to fine-tune your smaller organizational patterns to make sure that they are working effectively and in harmony with each other and the overall thematic approach.

One of the most familiar organizational patterns is *chronological order* and its variation, *in medias res*. You have been using these patterns since you were a small child in school telling what happened to you during the day.

Using chronological order requires only that you begin at the beginning and follow events through their actual sequence.

Chronological Order

THESIS: *The most important single event in my high school career happened on an otherwise uneventful day in the September of my senior year.*

TOPIC: The day began with my turning off the alarm clock and going back to sleep instead of getting up easily as I normally did.

TOPIC: It continued with the bus forgetting to stop at my stop (as usual) and my being late for my first class.

TOPIC: Football practice came all too soon.

TOPIC: The trip to the hospital seemed to take forever.

TOPIC: My career was over for the season.

Chronological order leads the reader clearly and effectively through a chain of events. At the same time, it is an easy pattern for a writer to use, either for the whole theme or for a paragraph or two.

The same story can be told with quite a different effect using the *in medias res* pattern. Rather than starting a story at the beginning of the action, the *in medias res* (Latin for "in the middle of the thing") pattern starts just before the climax, comes back for the details of the beginning, and then moves to the climax. This pattern is very often used in fiction.

In Medias Res Order

THESIS: *The most important single event in my high school career happened on an otherwise uneventful day in the September of my senior year.*

TOPIC: Football practice came all too soon that day.

TOPIC: You'd expect what happened to me on a day that began with my turning off the alarm clock and going back to sleep.

TOPIC: And the bus not coming and me being late to my first class.

TOPIC: The trip to the hospital seemed to take forever.

TOPIC: That ended my career for the season.

An *in medias res* pattern has the advantages of a more exciting beginning (because it starts closer to the heart of the action) and a faster tempo than chronological order. It also keeps you from being drawn too deeply into trivia in the beginning of your theme, as you might be in chronological narration when you set the stage at the beginning of your theme. Of course, both chronological order and *in medias res* can be used as patterns for the whole theme or for its parts, and both are very useful when you are telling what happened or how to do something or how you came to understand an idea—in short, in any situation in which narration (story telling) is appropriate.

Description (telling what something looks like or feels like or sound like and so on) can present a more difficult writing situation than narration. Except in writing classes, *telling* what something looks like is not a common assignment. Under most circumstances, if you wanted another person to be able to recognize Aunt Martha or your family home or your favorite tree or a geometric figure, you would use a picture, not an essay, as your teaching device. Yet the ability to describe clearly and simply is worth developing because description helps bring an argument to life. It helps the reader understand what it felt like to be there.

Your job as you describe something becomes one of selecting pertinent details, an organized pathway for the eye to follow, and appropriate labels for orders, sizes, shapes, and so on. Telling details, analogies, comparisons, and contrasts will help the reader sense the situation. A logical pathway (right to left; around the room; from the base of the lamp to its top; from the outside of the house to the inside) will help the reader follow the discussion. And exact labels (a circle with a circumference of 27 inches) will help the reader visualize what you are saying.

Front (of Farm) to Back Order

THESIS: *Father's farm presents an unbroken view of the abundance of nature.*

TOPIC: As you enter the property, you see great fields of corn.

TOPIC: As you move towards the house down the path, you see an orchard.

TOPIC: As you move towards the barn, you see the vegetable garden.

TOPIC: As you leave the back of the property, you see the abundance of neighboring farms.

In this case the student writer chose to follow a pathway that began at the farm entrance and moved step by step to the back of the property. Each topic sentence discussed what the reader would 'see" at that particular place, and each related to the thesis concept—"an unbroken view of the abundance of nature."

The writer might have chosen another pathway, perhaps making a better development in so doing. As with your other themes, your descriptive themes will benefit from some experimentation on your part, not only with the details that you will present but also with the patterns that hold them together.

Your expository themes—those in which you explain a concept clearly and concisely and at the level of difficulty that is appropriate for the audience you want to reach—have probably incorporated elements of narration and description. If not, you will now want to begin adding these patterns to your writing repertoire to help bring your ideas to life for your readers. All it takes is a paragraph or two of narration and maybe a few sentences of description to add punch and verve to your themes.

Most of your writing to date has been expository: You have been asked to select and limit a worthwhile topic and to develop and order subordinate material to express your ideas precisely. And you have probably already noticed that an expository theme is like a set of instructions for understanding an idea. It is not exactly a cookbook recipe, but it is like one in that you must provide your reader with the ingredients (concepts) for understanding, and you must provide them in the proper order so that everything you say makes sense and the proper results are achieved. If you skip steps, your reader might understand— or might come to a conclusion different from your own. The same is true if your steps are out of order.

Expository themes commonly rely on one of several patterns for their overall structure. Subparts of themes—such as paragraphs or paragraph clusters—may be governed by still other patterns. For example, your overall structure might follow a "how to" order, providing information in an appropriate sequence so that the reader can follow instruction to complete a process or perform a job ("how to" order, thus, is most like a cookbook recipe). At the same time, one paragraph might be governed by one of the narrative orders and another paragraph by a descriptive order.

The most important things about using a "how to" sequence are analyzing your audience (What does this audience already know about the concept? At what level must this discussion be pitched?), presenting your material in the appropriate sequence ("how to" order is thus related to chronological order), and making sure not to skip steps.

THESIS: *Starting an argument with your spouse is not a difficult task once you know how.*

TOPIC: Begin by figuring out what your opposite number finds irritating or threatening or somehow unpleasant.

TOPIC: Watch to discover the times of day or night at which your spouse is least likely to "have it together."

TOPIC: At the appropriate moment, say or do just the wrong thing; try to choose a time when your spouse is under some outside pressure (such as the need to complete an important project), since that facilitates the process.

THESIS: *You can do well at a job interview if you follow a few simple steps.*

TOPIC: Find out something about the company before going.

TOPIC: Dress appropriately for the company and the job for which you are applying.

TOPIC: Be prepared to talk about yourself and your qualifications for that job.

TOPIC: Be prepared to ask questions about the company and your responsibilities and future.

TOPIC: Rehearse the interview with a friend so that you get some practice asking questions and responding to them.

TOPIC: Do your best, and don't worry.

TOPIC: Follow up with a "thank you" letter if that is appropriate.

If you choose or are assigned to write a theme using the "how to" order, your greatest challenge will be in the preliminary analysis of audience and subject, since once you yourself know "how to" perform the process you will describe, the theme's structure pretty much takes care of itself. However, you will find yourself tempted to skip steps that are obvious to you (and not necessarily to your reader) or to take them out of order because you happened to think of them that way (if so, correct the sequence as you revise). And it is tempting to choose a topic, such as the process of writing a theme, that is too complex to describe properly in a theme of 500 or 1,000 or even 10,000 words. You will have to remember to limit your topic.

Another common expository order, and one that is often used in textbooks, is "easy to complex." This order is appropriate if your material is difficult or highly technical and you determine that your reader would need a foundation of basics on which to build an understanding of your ideas. You are not talking down to your reader by any means, but you are providing necessary background information so that your concepts are clear.

THESIS: *Although no one knows precisely what electricity is, we can both use it and describe its effects.*

TOPIC: Understanding electricity begins with a knowledge of the atom.
  1. The atom is like a miniature solar system, with electrons orbiting the nucleus like planets orbiting the sun.
     a. An electron is . . .
     b. The nucleus is . . .
  2. Electrons orbit in concentric rings called "bands."
     a. There are up to_____bands.
     b. They fill up with electrons according to . . .
     c. It is the outer or "conduction" band that is important to the discussion of electricity because electrons in this band can be made to flow as current.

TOPIC: Certain substances, known as *conductors,* give up their electrons easily.
  1. Conductors provide a pathway for the current.
  2. Many metals are conductors.

TOPIC: Other substances, called *insulators,* have few free electrons.
  1. Insulators confine current to its pathway.
  2. Substances such as glass, wax, and many plastics are insulators.

TOPIC: To produce electricity, all we have to do is spin metal coils inside a magnetic field.
  1. We are not sure how the magnetic field excites the electrons.
  2. But we do know that the faster we spin the coil (up to the limits of

toleration of the equipment), the higher the voltage of current we can generate.

An outline like this one assumes that the reader has probably heard words like *electron* and *voltage* before but is not quite sure of their meaning. To be consistent in this evaluation of the reader's knowledge, the writer would also have to explain any other technical terms (such as *magnetic field*) or provide a glossary that does so. Otherwise, the reader is likely to follow the discussion only as far as the fourth topic sentence and then become lost.

If the writer assumes a more knowledgeable audience, then most of the introductory material could be dropped and a far different development would be appropriate.

THESIS: *Although no one knows precisely what electricity is, we can both use it and describe its effects.*

TOPIC: The conduction band in the atom is central to generation of electric current.

TOPIC: Useful electricity requires conductors and insulators.

TOPIC: We produce electricity by spinning metal coils inside a magnetic field.

TOPIC: Transmission of electricity requires specialized equipment.

TOPIC: It is the distribution section that leads to the home.

If you are not sure how your audience will react to your specific topic, it is probably better to begin with a brief review of basics (or to provide it parenthetically or in footnote or glossary form) than to risk losing them by starting with material that is too difficult.

Your skill in analyzing your audience will be especially critical to the success of your *argumentative* themes: themes that deal with topics about which reasonable people can have differing points of view. In order to write a successful argumentative theme, you must bring your reader to understand your point of view (the goal of an expository theme), for without understanding, no agreement is possible. And if possible—and it is not always possible—you will bring your reader to agree with your beliefs. The attempt to do this will require you to use everything that you have learned about narration and description and exposition and everything that you have learned about logic and persuasion. In this regard it might be well to spend a few moments reviewing what you learned in Chapter 3 about evaluating arguments and points of view before you begin to practice the patterns common to argumentative themes.

You will be using three major patterns in your argumentative themes, two of which you saw in Chapter 3. You will use *deductive* order, *inductive* order, and *agreement* order, with your selection depending on your analysis of how hostile your audience is likely to be to your overall point of view. (Of course, you will be using the other patterns you have studied to control sections of your paper; you might, for example, begin with "easy to complex" for two paragraphs, proceed with chronological order for a paragraph, and move to a paragraph of narration—all within an overall argumentative pattern.)

Deductive order is the most direct approach, since you begin by stating your thesis sentence and then build a chain of evidence to support your point of view. Your goal is to keep your reader agreeing with you along the way so that your conclusion seems inescapable.

When you use an inductive pattern, you allow the evidence to come first, making your case by convincing your reader a little at a time and stating your thesis sentence only after your reader has been partially convinced. Agreement order is a variation of this and is used when the audience is likely to be genuinely hostile to your point of view. In this case you begin your theme by agreeing with some portion of an opposing argument in order to develop a mood of harmony and pleasantness before beginning on the argument itself. Your tone throughout the theme would be reasonable and dispassionate; you are a person who is "bending over backwards" to be fair, without, of course, becoming condescending or losing sight of "the truth" (your point of view) in the process.

The selection of an argumentative pattern is a deliberate choice that grows out of your audience analysis and your understanding of your material. It is made after you have developed your pro/con chart and after you have done the majority of your preliminary work on your topic. Thus, you may well come to your conclusions deductively (you have your point of view to start with; you are working to find the evidence necessary to prove that it is correct) and present them inductively, or vice versa. And the patterns do make a difference in the overall effect of your theme on your audience.

Deductive Pattern

THESIS: *America desperately needs a sensible, current energy policy like that proposed by Senator Jamison.*

TOPIC: Importing oil is a costly proposition.

TOPIC: Importing oil leaves us vulnerable to an embargo.

TOPIC: Even with imports, we will not have enough.

TOPIC: A problem like this is too great for local solutions to suffice.

TOPIC: We need a sensible national policy that accomplishes the following:
1. Sets priorities on energy usage.
2. Establishes a conservation ethic.
3. Establishes a conservation law.
4. Establishes goals for energy production.
5. Funds research and development of future energy sources for this country.

Inductive Pattern

TOPIC: Importing oil cost this country $_____ billion last year alone.

TOPIC: The last oil embargo cost $_____, and there's no predicting the impact of the next one.

TOPIC: If oil supplies run out, industry will be crippled and Americans will be without many products (drugs, plastics) that require oil as a raw material in their manufacture.

TOPIC: No local government can deal with a problem of this magnitude.

THESIS: *America desperately needs a sensible, current energy policy like that proposed by Senator Jamison.*

TOPIC: Such a policy would accomplish the following:
1. Set priorities on energy usage.
2. Establish a conservation ethic.
3. Establish a conservation law.
4. Establish goals for new energy production.
5. Fund research and development of future energy sources for this country.

Agreement Pattern

TOPIC: As everyone knows, the energy crisis is of great concern to all citizens of this country.
1. Higher and higher prices affect everyone.
2. Supplies become unavailable at any price.
3. Jobs are lost or curtailed because of the unavailability of supplies.

TOPIC: Our free-enterprise system has always handled this country's needs well.
1. The American standard of living is comparatively high.
2. Americans respond well to crises such as war and natural disasters.

TOPIC: It is true that problems become more and more complex.
1. Now other governments are involved in the supply of energy as well as our own.
2. The problem is nationwide, crossing state lines and industry lines as well.
3. The problem is political in that government officials are involved in energy production through policy making and through regulation.

THESIS: *Given all these factors, perhaps it would be best if the private companies that produce and deliver energy were controlled by the government.*

TOPIC: Of course, we would take steps to protect the interests of private citizens if we did this.
1. Shareholders would be reimbursed.
2. Oversight would be given to Congress in order to protect the public.
3. Officials in charge would be held accountable by election and other means.

TOPIC: At least in this way we have a chance at a workable energy policy.
1. Politicians would no longer "play with" the issue since they would be accountable.
2. Everyone would have to get together and work on the solution rather than bickering.
3. There would be a chance to coordinate efforts since control would be centered as would responsibility.

You will notice that the deductive pattern is straightforward, getting the work of the theme done quickly and without hesitation. The inductive pattern breaks the news gently to the reader, while the agreement pattern inches into it, almost never saying precisely what the writer means, and then, afterwords, quickly moves back to conciliation.

But no matter which pattern you select for your argumentative themes, you must still remember to apply all of the skills you have developed in your writing experience. It is sometimes tempting in the heat of argument to lose sight of the fact that understanding must come before agreement and that "being right" in and of itself does not convince your reader. Rather, it is your ability to write precisely, effectively, to the point, and tactfully when necessary that does the job for you.

EXERCISE 1

Select one of the following topics for another, with the consent of your instructor) and develop a 400- to 600-word theme using chronological order. Try to include at least a few sentences of description and a few of narration—more if possible. Then rewrite the theme using *in medias res* order. What kinds of details are changed, added, or eliminated by the change of pattern? How does the overall effect of the theme change? Be prepared to discuss the differences between your two themes in class.

TOPICS

1. The scariest day in my life
2. My best date
3. The funniest movie I ever saw
4. Me, the actor
5. My sports career
6. My biggest mistake

EXERCISE 2

Select one of the following topics (or another, with the consent of your instructor) and develop an expository theme using either "how to" or "easy to complex" order, depending on which is more appropriate for your topic and audience. Plan on about 600 to 800 words. You may subdivide the topics if you wish, and some research may be necessary in order to gather the facts you will need for your discussion. If you are doing research, be sure to subordinate your data to your thesis and topic sentences and to give proper credit to your sources of information.

TOPICS

1. Recharging a car battery
2. Preparing for midterms

3. How an electric heat pump works
4. How a gas furnace works
5. How thermal insulation saves energy
6. Acid rock music
7. Dipping a candle
8. Winning an argument

EXERCISE 3
Select an argumentative topic that if of interest to you (with the consent of your instructor) for a 500- to 800-word theme. Analyze your audience for this topic: Would the audience you envision be actively hostile, neutral, or in favor of your point of view? Select an argumentative order according to your audience analysis, and write the theme. For this assignment turn in your working papers, including your audience analysis, your statement of purpose, and so on. You may write a "letter to the editor" if you prefer.

EXERCISE 4
If you are like most people, when you are in an argument you rely, consciously or subconsciously, on the "fact" that "you are right." Even an analysis of the opposing points of view, such as that provided by a pro/con chart, will not sway you from your convictions.

You may find, however, that once this sense of rightness is taken from you, you argue more eloquently because you must rely on your sense of language and your sense of logic and even your sense of humor to make your points. So take the topic that you prepared for the previous exercise and write a 500- to 800-word theme arguing *against* your previous point of view. If you make a genuine attempt to "win the argument," you will learn a lot about the way arguments are made and especially about the way you yourself argue.

EXERCISE 5
Develop a 500- to 750-word theme assuming your audience to be your boss (you may invent a work situation if you wish) and your topic to be "I deserve a raise." Use "agreement" order for your theme. If you prefer, you may select another ordering pattern and use humor as you defend the thesis sentence "I do *not* deserve a raise." Your purpose in the second case would be to show, through the amusing way in which you express your ideas, that you are in fact deserving of more money.

3. Unity and Coherence

Unity is the singleness of purpose, content, audience analysis, tone (the writer's attitude toward a subject, whether serious or sarcastic or humorous or whatever), and style that marks the theme as an entity. *Coherence* is the internal connectedness that relates parts of the theme to each other and helps show the patterns of coordination and subordination through which the writer expresses ideas. Thus, unity and coherence are not synonymous, but they do relate to each other. A unified theme is more likely to be coherent than a disjointed one; similarly, the skills that put coherence into a theme are likely also to ensure unity. Thinking of a theme as an abstract structure may help you see how this is the case.

I believe that aberwags should be illegal in this state, for several important reasons. **1**

First, aberwags contribute to the problems we have been having with the mitavolic systems in the city. They increase the level of mackwed pollutants that are spewed into the air by factories, and they find their way into our water supply. **2**

Second, aberwags are costly to produce. They cost twice as much as witlanks and four times as much as mitvolls. Yet witlanks and mitvolls cause only slightly greater mitavolic problems than aberwags do. **3**

Finally, I believe that aberwags should be illegal in this state because they interfere with the right of the citizens to move freely through the areas in which they are built. Restricted areas such as those necessitated by aberwag production violate the sense of freedom for which America stands. There is no product that is worth that price. **4**

Even though you do not know what aberwags and mitavolic systems and mackwed pollutants and witlanks and mitvolls are, you can begin to discuss the structure of the theme. You realize that the entire theme stays with one purpose and one subject: The theme explains why the writer believes that aberwags should be illegal in this state. The tone remains reasonable and serious, but not somber. The sentence structure and vocabulary are clear and easy to understand, the unusual nouns notwithstanding. Apparently, the writer has decided that the intended audience did not need background explanation to understand this subject, and none is provided. Thus, this theme holds together: It is unified.

If you look more closely at the structure of the theme, you can see how the writer connected the parts. The thesis sentence concludes with the prepositional phrase "for several important reasons." That phrase promises a framework of discussion for the reader, who now has a right to expect the reasons to be listed and explained.

The second paragraph begins with a transition word, *first*. This tells the reader that the initial reason on the list is coming up. The third and fourth paragraphs also begin with transition words that mark the reader's (and the writer's) place in the discussion. Words like *similarly* and *on the other hand* and *nonetheless* perform the same function, helping the reader follow the writer's thought patterns. Of course, you use these words all the time in conversation.

The fourth paragraph, finally, uses another kind of transition. (The word *finally* in the preceding sentence is a transition word, telling you that this aspect of the discussion is about to end.) The topic sentence repeats the thesis sentence concept: "Finally, *I believe that aberwags should be illegal in this state.*" The repetition helps reinforce the main point, both by placement (since the conclusion is most likely to be remembered) and by repetition. Thus, the theme looks like Figure 13.

This theme is unified because it treats a single topic in a single manner. And it is coherent because the pathway and its connections are

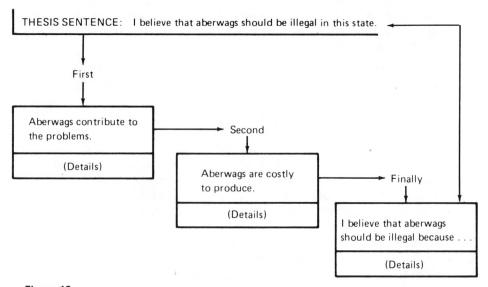

Figure 13

clearly set out for the reader to follow. To put it another way, if you think of a theme as a journey into an idea, unity is the control that keeps the writer and reader on the same journey, and coherence is the system of signs that marks the path. Both are related in that they help your theme make sense to your reader.

EXERCISE 1
Consider the following student compositions, deciding which are unified and which are not. Be prepared to discuss and defend your conclusions in class. Select a theme that is not unified properly and rewrite it to correct its faults.

A

Even before you apply for your first job, you should be aware that the world is a jungle. The people out there plan to use you to your fullest willingness to extend yourself and then throw you away when you are worn out.

Today, for example, I learned about a person who tried too hard once too often. That person committed suicide because he couldn't handle the one extra project.

If that happens to you, you are stupid because forewarned is forearmed and this discussion should be warning enough for anyone who isn't stupid. If you are applying for a job, or if you have one now, you should keep my warning in mind. Take it from an older and wiser person such as me and volunteer for nothing.

B

Even if you've never handled a needle and thread, you can learn to sew. This fact includes the gentlemen as well as the ladies.

Sewing requires just a few skills. First, you have to be patient, because, like most things, if you are not willing to do it right, you had best not bother at all. A garment poorly made is worse than none at all, so you must be willing to be precise. You need some space to work in, preferably space that can be devoted solely to your sewing so that you can leave your garment out until it is finished. It is very discouraging to have to clean up in the middle of a project so that the dining room table can be used for dinner.

Then it is a matter of selecting the materials to do the job with the pattern you have bought. You want to select the right pattern to start with because a too hard project initially can also be very discouraging and in fact can make you want give up sewing before you have really given it a fair try.

C

Managing money is my first priority right now. I am not a financial genius but have to be to get the job done. For example, right now I am trying to eat on $25.00 per week. Now, I know that that makes approximately $3.5714285 dollars per day, or a dollar for breakfast, a dollar for lunch and a dollar and change for dinner. What I haven't figured out is how to eat on that amount of money, especially since most of my meals must be purchased in restaurants (????). For that price, they aren't really restaurants.

I do enjoy spending my 39¢ a week allowance for recreation. That buys me a walk in the park, a bag of popcorn, and an ice cream bar every second week.

If other things don't seem important to me at times, it is because managing money is my first priority right now.

EXERCISE 2
Read the following student theme, underlining all the coherence devices that you can locate. How could the student have improved the unity and coherence of what she wrote? What else could be done to improve the theme?

Excellence in all that I do has always been very important to me as a person. I can remember when I was a small child in the first grade and I always had to have the neatest paper or the best grade or the most perfect attendance record.

Excellence too has marked my extracurricular activities. First, I am willing to put in all the time necessary to get a job done right, even if it means sleeping a little less that week. When I have the least important part in the play, I still have to be the best actress.

Finally, you need to understand that my commitment to being my very best is a permanent one. I intend to take this into the future. If you know me at all, you would understand what I mean and just how important excellence is to me.

EXERCISE 3

With the consent of your instructor, select a theme you have written for a previous class assignment and revise it, focusing your attention on developing more sophisticated patterns of organization and on the unity and coherence of the whole theme.

EXERCISE 4

Select one of the following "nonsense" topics. Develop it into a 400- to 600-word theme, inventing words where appropriate to keep the theme nonsense. Focus your attention on building a coherent structure, one in which the transition devices are strong enough to keep the reader on your theme's pathway, even though the pathway is not really going anywhere.

TOPICS

1. The wyerling process
2. Building a refloggitator
3. Emongs should be abolished
4. All people should be kilated at least once in their lives

chapter 6
paragraphs

1. Writing Effective Paragraphs

Paragraphs are thought compartments that serve as building blocks for your discussion when you write and as units of understanding when you read. In a well-written theme, each paragraph develops one specific chunk of the writer's world of ideas, and does so fully, specifically, and precisely. If they work well together, paragraphs progress in a sensible order from one to the next. They are unified and coherent.

Writing effective paragraphs means developing your ability to write and control topic sentences, make connections between ideas, use the kinds of paragraphs available to you to vary your style and the effect of your theme, and spend the time necessary to make each paragraph a full and satisfying experience for your reader.

As you will recall from your study of theme structure, your topic sentences are the main reasons you believe that your thesis sentence idea is true. They pass what we have called the "test of because."

THESIS: Buses are not the solution to this city's transportation problem
BECAUSE
1. Not all people will ride buses.
2. Buses create problems as well as solving them.
3. Other solutions to the problem would be better.

You might even consider your thesis sentence and topic sentence ideas to be one gigantic single sentence yoked together with the word *because* between the thesis sentence part and its topic sentence supports.

THESIS: Buses are not the solution to this city's transportation problem—*because*—not all people will ride buses, buses create problems as well as solving them, and other solutions to the problem would be better.

The question then becomes, how do you get from a situation in which you have what you believe to be an effective thesis sentence and a convincing group of topic sentences to one in which well-developed paragraphs have been written to support each? The answer comes when you back up and review what you have been doing all along as you followed the writing process suggested in this book. If you have been following those procedures, you began by thinking about your topic, limiting it and defining it and listing ideas about it as you attempted to develop a thesis sentence.

TENTATIVE THESIS: Buses are not the solution to this city's transportation problems.

IDEAS: Buses are noisy. Buses pollute. Buses are either overcrowded or empty. Buses don't run on time. Buses don't interconnect properly. People would rather drive. A bicycle is often a feasible solution. Car pools work too. Experience last Thursday. Marjorie's experience last year. Subway systems in New York and Montreal.

Your next step would be to read through your list of ideas, grouping those that seem to belong together and subordinating those that act as supports for others. For example, some ideas in the preceding list offer alternate solutions to the transportation problem: They would be grouped together. If your experience last Thursday had to do with the fact that buses don't interconnect properly, that experience would be subordinated to the more general statement of fact as you see it. Your new list might look something like this:

IDEAS:
1. Alternate solutions to the transportation problem
   a. A bicycle is often a feasible solution.
   b. Car pools work too.
   c. Marjorie's experience last year (walking was faster).
2. Problems with using buses as the solution
   a. Buses are noisy.
   b. Buses pollute.

    c. Buses compete with cars for available space on roads and in parking places.

    d. Buses don't always run on time.

      i. Which means they can't interconnect properly

      ii. Experience last Thursday

    e. People would rather not use buses.

This second list of ideas is just one attempt to order and subordinate what you will say in your theme. In the process of working with the material, you will decide to delete some things, like the subway systems in New York and Montreal, and you will think of others, like the fact that buses crowd highways and parking lots. You are looking for the most effective major supporting points for your thesis sentence, for an ordering pattern that works for those supports, for the correct subordination pattern for your ideas, and in fact—though you may not be aware of it—for the details from which you will build your paragraphs. Your transitions come both as part of the structure you are building and as part of the paragraphs you will write.

Let us look at another topic, following the process of development from the preliminary writing steps the student took through the rough paragraphs she wrote, focusing on how she got from her idea list and topic sentence list to her paragraphs.

Working Papers—Theme Number 7

ASSIGNMENT: 600–1000-word theme, topic of choice, focus on strength of structure and quality of paragraphs.

TOPIC IDEAS: Hobby (piano); decorating apartment; current event; science and industry; major in college—why I plan to be a nurse. Will write about why I plan to be a nurse since topic is important to me, I already know about it, it is reasonably small, can control it by adding or subtracting details, and was a previous topic option I didn't select (it is probably an acceptable topic). Hobby and decorating apartment not important enough in my life; current event and science and industry too vague, require research, etc. I'm happy with my topic choice.

AUDIENCE: Average adult, though if I use medical terms, I may have to define them.

PURPOSE: To explain why I want to be a nurse, preferably using humor to get my points across and to show that I understand the potential problems in my choice of career.

IDEAS: Service to others. Science. Family in medicine or related fields. Job market OK. Allows working hours to be shifted so I can stay home with family later. Meet interesting people, both patients and doctors. Really needed. Can get involved in career, etc.

TENTATIVE THESIS: I selected a career in nursing for several major reasons: a chance to study subjects I like and to employ my studies in a career; a chance to be of service to others; and a chance to meet and interact with interesting people, both patients and hospital staff.

By the time this student has gotten to her tentative thesis sentence, she has already made several very important decisions about her topic, whether she meant to or not. Her tentative thesis contains the seeds of her topic sentence structure, as shown in Figure 14. Thus, she has al-

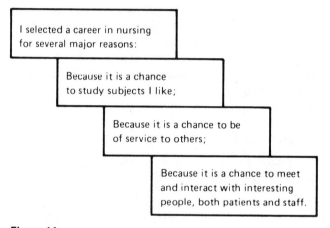

Figure 14

ready selected the major arguments from her idea list, and it is on the strength of these that her discussion will succeed or fail. She has said that her topic sentence ideas are essentially equal in weight and in importance to her—that is, that each reason for selecting nursing as a career is as important as every other reason—and she has selected an order of discussion for her theme. But she has yet to focus her ideas, to point attention to the most important reason, if there is one, and to subordinate other material. Let us return to her working papers and see how she does this.

Working Papers—Theme 7, Session 2

After a day away from the assignment, I see a problem with my tentative thesis sentence. All the ideas in it are not equally important to me. The part about studying really doesn't count as much as the other two ideas, and I guess if I'm going to be honest, the last part of the sentence is more compelling than the service ideal. So I will rephrase the thesis:

THESIS: All my life I have wanted to be a nurse although the reasons for that have changed as I have matured.

Yes—a more interesting approach. Now to the development:

TOPIC SENTENCES:
1. I first wanted to be a nurse after having read a book about Florence Nightingale (service ideal).
2. My studies confirmed my choice (I enjoy what I must learn and I do well).
3. But as I have matured, my main reason for going into nursing must be the fact that I will be working with and helping all kinds of people.
   a. Experiences as a candy striper.
   b. Family in medicine.
   c. People in nursing/medical profession on college staff.
   d. Perspective on life.

Most of the theme will be devoted to topic sentence 3. Now to the rough paragraphs:

My Career (Draft 1)

It seems that all my life I've wanted to be a nurse, although the reasons for that decision have changed as I have matured.

My "career" in nursing began not with the "doctor kit" I got for Christmas when I was five years old, but with a book I got out of the library when I was nine. It was a small book, but an important one to me. *Florence Nightingale: Nurse of the Crimean War* was picked up by accident because I wanted to know what kind of "crime" was involved in the "Crimean war" (honestly). Her story—the story of a woman who took nursing and made it into a profession—fascinated me. Few people know that before Florence Nightingale, nurses were considered on about the same level as prostitutes (which many of them were) and medical care for the wounded was almost nonexistent. Through nursing I thought that I too could make a contribution.

School work reinforced my decision. I have always liked sciences and done well in them. I am enjoying my nursing studies at the college and find the people involved in nursing to be fascinating. I have spent the last ten months as a candy striper at the hospital, and that experience has made me certain.

At the hospital, of course, I am low person on the totem pole. I don't assist in surgery and in emergency situations, I stay out of the way or try to comfort relatives. Mostly I read to people or write letters or carry things around. Sometimes I really get to help out. But I *am* there and I *do* see what is going on and I *am* needed. I am working with all kinds of people, helping them often at a very critical time in their lives. I interact with doctors and nurses, plumbers and teachers and housewives and small children and politicians. In very few careers does a person get a chance to be important in all these kinds of lives. It is for these reasons that I am sure that nursing is the right career for me.

To get from her topic sentence structure to draft one of the theme, this student simply told why her topic sentences were true. She said something about each of them and thus got paragraphs on paper. Her job as she revises becomes one of selecting the most pertinent details, cutting the less relevant material (for example, if the first topic sentence concept is really less crucial she should not have devoted so many words to the second paragraph), adding transitions, and tightening the overall structure. That may mean going back to rework the structure before polishing the paragraphs and sentences and diction, or it may simply entail moving details to put them in more emphatic positions. The general rule for theme writing is that the beginning of the theme should contain your second most emphatic argument or detail in order to pull your reader into your discussion, while the most vital argument should be reserved for last as the "clincher." Here is what this student did on her first revision:

To Be Needed (Revision 1)

Have you ever been really needed? Well I have, and I have selected a career in which I will have the opportunity to do the work I like, help people who really need help, and interact with people from all walks of life. I am going to be a nurse.

It all began by accident when I was nine years old and in the library. I saw a book about Florence Nightingale. Her life and work inspired me: If she could make a contribution, so could I. Then too, I've always enjoyed science and science related subjects and done well in them.

What decided me for sure, though, has been my experience as a candy striper in the hospital here. I won't try to fool you. I haven't delivered any babies or saved any lives, but I *have* helped people and met some fantastic (and not-so-fantastic) people.

Mostly what I do at the hospital is read to people, write letters, and run errands. But I see what is going on. I've interacted not only with the doctors and nurses but with the patients: plumbers and teachers and politicians and bus drivers and housewives (and one househusband) and small children. I've been there at a critical time in their lives and I've gotten close to them. I like the feeling of being needed, and I find what I am doing to be challenging and stimulating: just the characteristics I am looking for in my career. That is why I have chosen to be a nurse and why I am happy with my choice.

The revised theme focuses more closely on the student's major points, cutting unnecessary details and rearranging the concepts slightly to increase their impact. Some work still remains to be done on the theme. For example, the final paragraph would be more convincing if the student described at least one specific experience with a patient so that the reader could relate to the feelings she has about her career. The second paragraph now seems a little skimpy, covering the subjects too quickly: She could add details here (perhaps some of those she used in her rough draft). And transitions need to be added to make the whole thing flow smoothly.

EXERCISE 1

Consider the following student themes. Are they acceptable as rough drafts? If not, what would need to be done to them to make them into acceptable rough drafts? If they are acceptable rough drafts, what revisions would be needed to make them into polished themes? Select one of the themes and rewrite or revise it as necessary to make it a polished discussion. You may invent details if need be to accomplish your goals. Be prepared to discuss all of the themes in class.

A

Little Women

Little Women was the book which most influenced me.

Jo's life captured my imagination, even though I was the oldest child and she was the second oldest. Ever since I've read that book, I have wanted to be a writer.

Though I haven't done too well in this composition class to date, I am working hard and improving. I have written several short stories and many poems, and even sold some of them to small magazines. I intend to have a career writing fiction and drama.

My preparation for this career includes a major in English and a minor in theatre arts. I think I will do well.

B

Alert but Undecided

My problem is that I like to read. So many books have influenced me that I can't really point to one of them, especially for a career choice. And I have not yet decided on a career.

My plan is this:

I am tentatively majoring in business administration, since that gives me a broad range of options (and more electives in the first year than most other majors). During my freshman year, I am exploring various career fields, both through my use of electives and by going out into the community. I am keeping my eye on the classified advertisements to see what is usually available and what is scarce. I am talking with business people for advice (most will talk with you if you seem intelligent, know what you want, and are willing to respect their schedules) and to cultivate contacts for future opportunities. In short, I am undecided but alert in my career field and an eclectic and happy reader.

C

A Sci-Fi Freak

If you think science fiction is moon maidens and martian monsters dressed in green, two things are true: You are right, it was and is, and second, you have been away from it a while. Science fiction today is an incredibly sophisticated place of infinite possibilities and worlds, something to capture the spirit, engage the intellect, widen the horizons. You are speaking with a genuine sci-fi freak.

I can't say that one book has influenced me more than any other. I am not an "influenceable" person in that sense and I don't use reading material to be influenced in terms of a career. I do use it to learn about various possibilities, to think, and to expand my horizons. And of course, being a sci-fi freak, I read for pleasure. While I can't, then, say that I have selected a career from reading a book, I can say that books have been and will remain important in my life.

EXERCISE 2
Select a topic that interests you and consider your thought processes as you move through the stages from initial conception to finished theme. Where do you have problems? Insofar as you can tell, what causes those problems? Can you work them out? Keep a journal of your thoughts and decisions (similar to the working papers in this chapter) and turn that in with your finished theme. Plan on 500 words.

2. Developing Your Paragraphs

Effective paragraphs say enough about their topic sentences so that the reader is satisfied that the concept has been explored fully and so that the relevance of the topic sentence concept to the thesis sentence and to other paragraphs in the theme has been made clear. Only material relevant to that topic sentence remains in the paragraph, and the paragraph does not provide so much information that the reader becomes bored.

You will find that developing your paragraphs will be one of the "fun" things about writing. If you have followed your rough-draft procedures and done some overall revising, your theme structure should be set. You already have a firm idea of what you want to say and its focus. Your rough paragraphs are in place. What remains now is discussing the details, the lively experiences, the intriguing facts, the pertinent statistics, all of which are already in your possession in most cases or, in others, easily located on a library reference shelf or somewhere else. You will probably find that while your topic sentences are likely to grow out of your rough-draft procedures, paragraph development is in most cases a function of the revising process in which you stop to consider the perfection of each part of your theme.

Consider the following student themes:

A

A Day in the Sun

After the rigors of final exam week, I really enjoyed my day in the sun.
Yesterday I went to the beach in the morning. I had lunch on the sand.
On my way home I stopped off at the store to pick up one or two things.
While there, I met a friend I had not seen in a long time.

Then I went and played a game of volleyball with some friends. The
day concluded with a barbecue in the backyard.

B

Flight

*What I did for relaxation after final exam week was something which I
really enjoy and which relatively few people ever do—I piloted an airplane.*
I got interested in flying when I was very young. No one in my family
liked planes, or anything like that. I guess I was just a dreamy kid who
liked to look up. What I saw fascinated me.

An airplane meant two things together—freedom from where and who
I was, for when I was in the plane, I was above myself, and power to control a mass of metal and wire and power to go many places and do many
things. So I read everything I could about the subject. And that's how I got
interested in airplanes.

C

Dachshollow

For relief from final exam week, I bought a puppy.
Since my favorites have always been miniature dachshunds, that is
what I selected. I bought the puppy at a place called Dachshollow. Dachshollow is a hyphenated word in its meaning, if not its spelling. The
"Dachs" part is for dachshunds; the hollow is the place itself, a niche in
the woods away from civilization.

Dachshollow has two kinds of dogs—miniature dachshunds, as you
might expect, and something you would not expect—Great Danes. The
miniature dachshunds have the run of the place during the day, but it be-

longs to the Danes at night. They guard the half acre and the lady who owns the place—assisted by the yapping of their miniature friends.

Your reaction to the first theme was probably that the paragraphs were sketchy, that somehow the experience of a "day in the sun" was not conveyed. Details were missing, and there was no attempt to portray the place or the sensory impact of it. Sketchy paragraphs are a common problem with rough drafts, and should be repaired in the revision process.

A1

My Day in the Sun

After the rigors of final exam week, I really enjoyed my day in the sun.
The day broke clear and crisp, unlike the hazy mornings of the previous week. I arose at dawn, dressed quietly, and drove the four miles from our house to the beach. I was early and had the road and the countryside to myself.

I wanted a chance to be alone to think, and the silence of the morning and the emptiness helped. The beach is always lonely before about 9 A.M. I like it that way.

By the time the day warmed up and the people started to come, I was already calm and within myself. The warm sand, the cool water, and the hot sun soothed away final exam nerves. The rhythmic motion of the water and its magnitude always make me feel like a part of something bigger than myself and in so doing make my otherwise large problems fall into their proper perspective.

The revised version of this theme is substantially different from the rough draft. Details have been added to explain exactly what happened on the day and how the writer was affected by the experience. The important part of the experience—the morning—was expanded; the rest of the experience (the store, the barbecue, the volleyball game) was eliminated.

The second student theme, "Flight," has enough details in the paragraphs, although more exciting details might have been selected, but it wanders away from the subject promised in the title and the thesis sentence. The main concept is not flight so much as how the student came to be interested in airplanes. As with the sketchy paragraphs in the first theme, this one too will require some substantial reworking if the student plans to stay with the thesis sentence idea. It would be less trouble to rewrite the thesis sentence and title to suit the subject matter actually treated in the theme.

B1

How I Got Interested in Airplanes

What I did for relaxation after final exam week was something I really enjoy—I renewed my long interest in studying airplanes.

I became intrigued by flying and airplanes when I was very young. No one in my family was a pilot or anything like that. I guess I was just a dreamy kid who liked to look up. When I did, I saw airplanes. They fascinated me, and I had to know what made them fly.

That led me on a quest to libraries and air and space museums, to flight schools at local airports and to conning rides on small planes out of pilots in exchange for mowing lawns and washing windows and whatever else a 12-year-old could do. And I was never sorry, either for the physical labor or for the studying I did.

Airplanes are mechanical, but they are also magic. They are mechanical because they have engines and struts. They require fuel and maintenance. They are built on assembly lines. But they are also more than the sum of their parts, which is what makes them magic. The instant when the plane takes the air, when it becomes itself rather than a thing on the ground, is a magician's dream, and what makes all of the studying worthwhile.

B2

Flight

What I did for relaxation after final exam week was something which I really enjoy and which relatively few people ever do—I piloted an airplane.

There is only one word for airplanes—magic. If you've never been in a small plane, you couldn't possibly understand. You are on the ground. Then, suddenly, the plane takes the air, and everything is different. The rules. The perspectives. Everything. And if you are the pilot, only your best is good enough—because your life and the lives of others depend on it.

For me it is the instant of take-off which makes the study and the expense and the effort of flying worth it. No other experience in my life is quite like that transition. It is an experience which I would recommend to you. For myself, I realize that flying can be dangerous. But if I have to die, it would be worth it. That's how much being a pilot means to me.

The theme about Dachshollow also gets sidetracked. The title promises a discussion of the place, but the thesis sentence promises a theme about buying a puppy. The theme in fact is about both, with neither idea subordinated to the other. The problem is most acute in the second paragraph, which begins with the idea of miniature dachshunds and moves from there to Dachshollow, the place of purchase, and then to the meaning of the name itself. Revising the theme required that the student subordinate one idea or the other and that each paragraph be carefully structured to treat one topic sentence component.

C1

Dachshollow

For relief from final exam week, I bought a puppy—but it is the story of the place where I bought that puppy, Dachshollow, that I really want to tell.
Dachshollow and I met by coincidence, an odd advertisement in the classified section of the newspaper at a time when I was scanning regularly for miniature dachshund puppies, and a phone call answered by a pleasant woman who said that she was out in the country a ways, but we were welcome to come down. She was out in the country, two hours' worth, and so far that she did not have a street number for Dachshollow, just a street.

I followed her directions carefully since I have a penchant for getting lost. It was pretty country I drove through. Though I am not normally patient on long trips (two hours is long for me to be in a car), this day was relaxing.

After I had made my final turn and driven the two miles as instructed, I saw a wooded area with a small, dilapidated house and a run of kennels. That, thought I, must be the place—until I saw the dogs. A dozen or more, and they were Great Danes, not miniature dachshunds. I drove by slowly. The only other dog on the place was a German shepherd aggressively defending the area.

I figured I was lost, as usual, so I retraced my steps until I got to the country store (really) from which I called Mrs. Peters. When she finally answered, she said that I hadn't been lost at all, and to come on back.

Great Danes and miniature dachshunds—the one as big as a pony, and the other just a handful—share the world of Dachshollow. Together they are cared for by and themselves take care of a woman who has abandoned the rat race where final exams are necessary to do what she loves: raise and show and sell dogs. The big ones and the small ones fill different needs for her. The place, Dachshollow, is her world.

The house isn't much, barely shelter. The Danes have outside runs with large dog houses for bad weather and for the puppies. The miniature dachshunds, less hardy than their larger friends, have the best housing of all. The dogs share the woods and the grounds. The miniature dachshunds have the run of the place during the day, but it belongs to the Danes at night. They guard the half acre and the lady whose dream it is—assisted by the yapping of their miniature friends.

When themes get sidetracked during the rough-draft procedures, the problem usually rests with the topic sentences and with the amount of care given to developing, analyzing, and organizing them. If they are not sufficiently well thought out in advance, the theme will skip from idea to idea, as the rough draft of "A Day in the Sun" did, without really discussing any; or it will end up discussing something other than the thesis sentence, as the rough draft of "Flight" did; or it will try to discuss more than one main idea as the initial version of "Dachshollow" did. It is harder to revise if your initial writing procedures have not been performed carefully.

EXERCISE 1
Turn to the "Letters to the Editor" section of your newspaper and examine the kinds of letters that appear there. Can you pick out the thesis sentence idea in each? Do the paragraphs build a structure of support for that main idea? Evaluate each paragraph of the best letter. Is it developed fully enough so that you as a reader are satisfied with the discussion? How does the effectiveness of the development influence your judgment about the issue?

Select one of the letters and revise it, correcting any deficiencies and improving it where you can in terms of adding more pertinent details (which you may invent as need be) and other developmental material. You may, if you prefer, select an issue that is of concern to you and prepare your own "letter to the editor."

EXERCISE 2
Evaluate the following student theme in terms of the characteristics of proper development that you have studied in this chapter. Then revise

it (inventing developmental material if necessary) so that in your judgment it is an effective argument for its point of view. If you prefer, you may write a 500- to 750-word theme or letter to the editor developing your own point of view on this topic.

Making It in School

I have always been a person who "made it" in school. That is, I got along with the teachers and most other students. I moved from grade to grade as appropriate. I participated in extracurricular activities without getting overwhelmed by them. And I got good marks in the subjects which interested me and in those which did not. Yet I feel that what I needed to do to "make it" in school was somehow detrimental to me as a person.

Making it in school requires subordinating your own personality to the needs of the system. You never can do what you want. You always must do what you are told.

Being quiet and passive were the qualities most rewarded. If you asked questions, you were praised, as long as the questions were what the teachers wanted asked. If you asked questions which you wanted to ask, you got in trouble.

My natural curiosity was also squelched.

That is why I feel that making it in school was detrimental to me as a person.

3. Paragraph Variety

Some paragraphs are very short.

Other paragraphs take a page or more, going into great detail on an important topic sentence. Both short and long paragraphs have a place in your theme, enhancing its appearance, its rhythm, and its impact. A short paragraph in a group of longer paragraphs will stand out as important, as will a massive paragraph in a theme that consists largely of short paragraphs. And there will be more to say about some topic sentences than about others. Just the simple physical process of varying the length of your paragraphs will help make your composition more interesting.

Variety is possible also in your use and placement of topic sentences. Like the thesis sentence in the theme, the topic sentence can start the paragraph, appear in the middle, or end the paragraph. And topic sentences can control more than one paragraph of discussion. Consider the following student paragraphs.

A

Learning to Write

I can't say that I was looking forward to learning how to write on the day that I first walked into my freshman composition class. For one thing, I had heard a lot about freshman comp., none of it good. **But my major concern was that writing has always been very difficult for me.**

My problems with writing probably began with grade school. I was never much of a student. Other things in life, like having fun and going places, seemed more important than sitting around in a classroom learning about Dick and Jane and Spot, or memorizing multiplication tables. Then too, I was frustrated because the things I could say in writing were so insipid compared with the things I was thinking and feeling.

Junior high school was no better in general and was specifically worse when it came to writing. Now we focused our attention on such useful things as the intricacies of outline form and the motives of Hamlet. I still haven't seen the usefulness of outline form. My objections to Hamlet were that I was far too young to consider "being and not being." The upshot was that my writing grades were none too good, which did not bolster my confidence much.

By the time I got to high school, I had already given up on my writing career. I was assigned such topics as "George Washington, Father of Our Country" and "How I Spent My Summer Vacation" and "The American Political System." From what I've learned in this class, I realize that part of my problem with writing in high school was that the teachers didn't know much more than I did (consider the topics assigned), though I did have some good teachers and some good topics. But it was a matter of too little and too late. Thus, I already had a negative attitude about writing before I even got into freshman composition. Writing had always been difficult and not at all worth the bother.

B

Learning to Write

I don't mean to offend anybody, but you don't learn to write in school—not in public school, and not in college. **If you learn to write at all, and most people never do, you will learn it in life.**

The kinds of writing you do in schools are not relevant to what you need in life. The world outside asks that you be able to fill out a job application, not that you write a 500-word composition about a poem. The world outside asks that you be able to deal effectively with complicated issues; student themes ask that students deal with inanities or else that they handle abstractions ("Define the Nature of 'Good'") with no relevance to anything except the need to keep a professor employed.

Even those student themes and paragraphs which pretend to teach you "some of the skills you will need" to succeed in life fall short of the mark. You may learn a skill here. You may master a skill there. But never do you pull the whole thing together. Never do you do something relevant.

If you learn to write at all, you learn it on the job or at your desk at home.

On the job you learn to communicate with real people about issues which may not matter in the great scheme of things but which count that moment. You learn the language which works—often not the formal stuff from school. And you learn to be brief or else so long and complicated that you scoot by without having your message read (your original intent in that case).

At home, if it is worth it to you, you struggle with the nouns and verbs which make it come alive for you, and with the issues which touch your own life. You are your own harshest critic because in the end you are the only one who really cares if you learn to write. I am not saying that your instructors don't care and don't put in a lot of time grading your papers and making suggestions to you. Sometimes I can tell that the teacher put in more time on my paper than I did. But the point is that the teacher has at least 25 other students and probably more like 75 others. And you will be gone in a few weeks. So if you don't care about your writing, no one does.

And the truth is that most people don't care. Writing is a complicated skill—like dancing or playing professional football—requiring more work than most people care to give it. Getting by is all that matters for most of us. Those of us who care to learn to write will do so—with the help of our teachers if possible, or in spite of them, if necessary.

In the first student theme, each paragraph begins with its topic sentence, with the framework for the theme looking like this:

THESIS: *But my major concern was that writing has always been very difficult for me.*
1. My problems with writing probably began with grade school.
2. Junior high school was no better in general and was specifically worse when it came to writing.

3. By the time I got to high school, I had already given up on my writing career.

The first paragraph introduces the idea of the theme, beginning by touching on secondary reasons why this student did not look forward to writing classes and concluding by stating the thesis sentence. The following three paragraphs proceed in chronological sequence through the student's writing career, providing experiences, details, and reasons to support each topic sentence. The topic sentences in turn support the thesis.

The second theme has a more complicated structure. It too begins its introductory paragraph with information other than its thesis sentence. But its skeletal structure reveals more use of subordination:

THESIS: *If you learn to write at all, and most people never do, you will learn it in life.*
1. The kinds of writing you do in schools are not relevant to what you need in life.
   a. What the world wants versus class assignments.
   b. You don't learn useful skills.
2. If you learn to write at all, you learn it on the job or at your desk at home.
   a. What you learn on the job.
   b. What you learn at home.
   c. You learn at home because you care.
   d. Or you don't learn because it doesn't matter to you.

In the second theme too each topic sentence controls several paragraphs of discussion (each of which has its own "subtopic" sentence), and one topic sentence stands as a paragraph by itself, highlighting its importance and varying the pace of the theme as a whole.

As you work to revise your own themes, you will want to experiment with the placement of your topic sentences and with the length and complexity of your paragraphs. There is no one way that is right all the time; you are looking for the best way to express your own ideas.

Part of being flexible as a writer is being willing to experiment with what you have written, to back up and try alternate ways of saying it. As you strive for greater perfection in your themes, you will want to use the many different kinds of paragraphs to add variety and depth to what you have to say. Paragraphs can be built around reasons, details (facts, statistics, and experiences, among others), quotations, and comparisons. Paragraphs can introduce and provide background information; they can argue or summarize; they can connect ideas, restate them, and conclude. In the "real world," of course, most paragraphs perform a mixture of these functions—an ordinary theme would be unlikely to have more than a paragraph or two built solely of reasons, for example. But for the purpose of learning how to write and use these paragraphs it is helpful to focus on each kind as an entity.

REASONS

Paragraphs that state reasons usually introduce a theme or conclude it, making the writer's major points.

A

I chose a career in medicine for three main reasons. First, I have always been interested in sciences, especially biology and chemistry. Second, I enjoy helping people, and medicine will give me a chance to do just that. And finally, I would like to enjoy the finer things in life, and a medical career will give me the remuneration which will allow me to do just that.

B

In conclusion, it is clearly evident that public employees should not be allowed to strike. In accepting a government job, they exchanged the right to strike for greater job security. In accepting a government job, they also accepted the rules prohibiting such action. And in accepting a government job, they undertook responsibilities, many of which, like fire and police protection, the community must have for its very survival. Thus, while it might be in their own personal interest to strike, it is in the interest of the greater number of people that they not be allowed to do so.

Paragraphs that consist solely of reasons are not usually very effective because they lack the details necessary to bring the topic to life for the reader. In fact, such a paragraph could provide the structural framework for a theme.

THESIS: *I chose a career in medicine for three main reasons.*
   1. First, I have always been interested in sciences, especially biology and chemistry.

2. Second, I enjoy helping people, and medicine will give me a chance to do just that.
3. And finally, I would like to enjoy the finer things in life, and a medical career will give me the remuneration which will allow me to do just that.

Each of these sentences would act as a topic sentence, controlling one or more paragraphs that would help clarify the idea for the reader.

DETAILS

Details are the specific descriptive elements that define and explain a thesis or topic sentence—in effect, they form the actual *content* of most paragraphs, explaining, clarifying, and defending ideas. Details include facts, statistics, and experiences as well as anecdotes, analogies, quotations, and comparisons (quotations and comparisons will be treated as separate sections here because of the special techniques needed to handle them well). It is the vibrancy of the details that brings paragraphs to life.

A

If you are looking for a reason to give up cigarettes, I can give you a couple. Fact: Smoking is an expensive habit. If you smoke one pack a day, it probably costs you about $300 for the pleasure, not counting any extra money you spend for dry cleaning or other related expenses. Fact: Smoking is an expensive habit. If you smoke, you are twice as likely to have a heart attack (if you are male or if you are female and past 40). Fact: Whether they know it or not, smokers inconvenience other people who breathe in the pollutants from the cigarettes. The general run-of-the-mill air already has more than they need.

B

According to the latest polls, only 10 percent of the American people have faith in the honesty of their government. The press does a little better, but not much: 23 percent believe in it. Corporate officers fare about as well as the press: 21 percent of the public think that they are telling the truth—some of the time. Clearly, either this country has become a nation of cynics, or, and this is more likely, it is time to examine the validity of our opinion polls.

C

"Tell Grandpa not to worry about me. I'll be all right."

My first experience of death was not totally unexpected. Eileen had been sick all of her life; she had cystic fibrosis. If you don't know what that is, suffice it to say that it is a disease which makes breathing very difficult, and one which is normally fatal, as it was in Eileen's case, before adulthood. But Eileen was ten.

Until the last, she was patient and uncomplaining, always more considerate of others than of her own problems. It was just for a check-up, a routine part of her life, that she went to the hospital that Thursday. But she kept getting weaker and weaker. It was as if her body gave up. But when I think of her, that's not what I remember. I remember her looking up and seeing how upset my grandfather was that the child would die first. I will always remember her telling Grandpa not to worry. And I will always hope that—somewhere—she is all right.

You can draw the details that fill paragraphs from an almost unlimited number of sources: from your own experiences or imagination; from the experiences of others; from what you've learned in school or on the job; from any number of reference books or textbooks. For the paragraphs to have the greatest impact, however, you will need to select the most pertinent parts of an experience to relate or the most striking fact or statistic to make your point. And you will need to portray them specifically so that the reader will understand what you have to say and relate to your point of view.

QUOTATIONS

In most college themes quotations will be used in one of three ways: to get attention, to clinch a point, or to support an argument in a research paper. In all of these cases, the quotation must be relevant; its source must be cited; and of course it must be correctly quoted. It will take special practice to learn to introduce quotations smoothly and to subordinate them to whatever argument they are intended to support.

A

"The most certain test by which we judge whether a country is really free," according to the historian Lord Acton, "is the amount of security enjoyed by minorities." For the freedom to have meaning, the security must apply to all minorities, whether or not they are popular in the current mentality of the country or whether or not the majority abhors their point of view. For that reason, I believe that communists should be allowed to speak on campus.

B

Most discussions of patriotism focus around whether or not a certain person is a "patriot" or a certain act is "patriotic." But there is a more fundamental question to be resolved: Is patriotism in and of itself beneficial or is it harmful?

> These are the times that try men's souls. The summer soldier and the sunshine patriot will, in this crisis, shrink from the service of his country; but he that stands it NOW, deserves the love and thanks of man and woman.

Our country has been nurtured on words like this famous statement by Thomas Paine in 1776 (*American Crisis,* no. 1, December 19, 1776). Yet there is another point of view. Listen to George Bernard Shaw: "You'll never have a quiet world till you knock the patriotism out of the human race." And again, Shaw: "Patriotism is a pernicious, psychopathic form of idiocy." And Arthur Schopenhauer: "Patriotism is the passion of fools and the most foolish of passions."

Many famous men have expended many words on the subject of patriotism. It is one well worth our consideration and a closer look. . . .

COMPARISONS

When you *compare*, you show how two or more things are alike; when you *contrast*, you show how they are different. But even in contrasting, some essential points of similarity are taken for granted; for example, you would not be likely to contrast a Volkswagen with a beach ball, but it does make sense to contrast one make of car with another. Whether you are comparing or contrasting (or doing both), you will want to proceed in a logical, point-by-point fashion through your topic. The charts that you learned to make in the early chapters of this book will help you develop your evidence.

A

Uncle Steve is very much like the pioneer and folk hero Davy Crockett. Neither of them was much on neighbors, and both lived for whatever adventure they could squeeze out of life.

B

The success I have had on our high school football team depended on the same personal qualities which I hope will make me a success in my chosen field—business.

First and foremost, being a high school football star required determination. I know that from the outside the game looks like a "glory trip." But from the inside, it is tough work—and toughest when you most want to do something else for a change instead of practicing or getting in shape.

From what I've learned about business in my first few months in college, it is just that kind of determination which will be needed in my career. Even though the tackling in business is not likely to be literal, it will be painful nonetheless. I am sure there will be times when I would rather go to a movie (or a football game) than finish a project. But it is the project I will complete.

My high school football taught me to take punishment, both physical and mental, without whimpering or giving up. This lesson too will stand me in good stead in my future career. In any business environment, there will be times when you lose a sale through no fault of your own or when a "friend" turns out to be not so good a friend after all. If you don't expect it, and if you don't *know* you can take it, you are likely to get discouraged. I know I can take it.

And finally, my high school football taught me to play as part of a team, to adjust to the various personalities and the moods of other people, and to get the job done nonetheless. The relevance of these skills to the business world is clear and really needs no explanation.

Comparisons can be more or less obvious, but it is important to select the main elements of each item to be compared and not to ignore a major point that might invalidate what you are saying. To be effective at all, a comparison must fit perfectly and must clarify and elucidate the idea under discussion.

PLANNING FOR PARAGRAPH VARIETY

You can plan your paragraph variety as part of your rough draft procedures at the point where you are organizing your ideas and evidence.

THESIS: *This country needs nuclear energy if we are to meet our electricity demands in this century.*

I. America is an energy-hungry nation.

Reason A. Industry uses _____ percent of our energy to sustain the economy.

Fact 1. The steel industry alone uses _____ percent.

Example 2. During the last oil boycott and the resulting energy shortage . . .

Reason B. The American consumer shows no signs of being willing to make the sacrifices necessary to cut our energy use enough.

Fact/ Example 1. Conservation efforts, while genuine in intent are minimal in impact.

Fact 2. Our energy use per capita doubles every _____ years.

Fact 3. Last year alone, each person in America used the equivalent of-_____ barrels of oil.

Quotation 4. The President said, "Americans . . ."

II. Without nuclear energy, we will not be able to meet our energy demands.

Reason A. Supplies of oil are diminishing.

Fact 1. How much we once had.

Fact 2. How much we have now.

Reason B. Coal alone cannot meet our energy needs in a satisfactory fashion

Fact 1. Strip mining in West Virginia has created a new set of problems to be solved.

Fact 2. Transporting coal is a problem, given the state of our railroad systems.

Fact 3. Coal can easily supply_____percent of our energy needs in the next century.

Fact/ Argument 4. If we want coal to supply another _____%. we will have to implement the following programs . . .

III. Other sources of energy such as solar and geothermal energy have their problems.

Fact A. New and largely experimental.

Fact B. Costly.

Fact/Argument C. Actual implications and impact on environment untested.

IV. Only nuclear energy has current potential to solve energy problems, but we must act immediately.

Fact/Argument A. Technology developed, tested.

Fact B. But it takes a very long time to build a nuclear-power plant.

To plan your paragraph variety in this fashion, you need not have your actual data in hand (as long as you have enough knowledge to be fairly sure that the data, once gotten, will support your argument), and you don't need to have your examples or quotations ready. You simply leave a slot for that kind of paragraph, or paragraph series, and plan to fill it as you do your research and prepare your rough drafts and work out your revisions.

INTRODUCTORY PARAGRAPHS

The introductory paragraph or paragraphs of a theme perform a variety of functions. They get interest, using an anecdote, a quotation, a striking fact or statistic. They can provide background information: the history of an issue, the basic concepts necessary for a reader to understand the thrust of the theme, or definitions if they are needed. Introductory paragraphs show the general relevance of the topic and thesis to the reader and to the larger world. They focus on a topic and state a thesis sentence.

A

Joseph McPherson is an average man. He works hard for his money. He has a family—one wife and two children. He goes to church, not every Sunday, but regularly. He graduated from high school and had 2 years at a junior college. There is not much that is different about Joe—except that once or twice a year, he has a compulsion to gamble. And during those one or two weeks, so much havoc is wreaked upon his financial situation and his family life that Joe requires special help from relatives to feed and clothe his family and he requires special counseling from professionals to put his family life back together.

It would be reassuring to think that Joe McPherson is unique in his problem, or that it affects only a few other people. But facts state otherwise. Over _____people in the United States today suffer from the compulsion to gamble, according to the Department of Health, Education and Welfare. For _____percent of them, the problem is so disruptive that special help must be sought. The cost to the economy for the special, tax-funded help alone is $_____per year. Of course, that does not begin to measure the other costs: the emotional damage to families, the loss of self-respect, the destruction of careers.

Joe McPherson and all of those like him can be helped if the government is willing to implement the program proposed by Senator Byner in a campaign speech to this student body. . . .

B

For thousands of years, people cooked their food with heat, but now, for the first time, they can cook with electromagnetic waves.

Microwaves and the ovens which bear their name open up two new dimensions in cooking: They run more cheaply than ordinary electric ranges and they cook more quickly. . . .

C

I suppose you assume that you will never grow old. At nineteen, I must admit that I feel that way, even though part of my mind tells me that facts are otherwise. Still to marry, to raise a family, still to settle into a career or even buy a first new car, it is hard for my generation to feel much concern for the problems of the elderly. Yet *now* is the time to begin to solve those problems so that they won't be yours when it is your turn to be old.

We can make a beginning in the process of solving the problems of the elderly by . . .

D

How many centimeters are there in a meter? How do meters relate to miles, and what is the relationship between kilograms and ounces?

Before too long, the American people will have to puzzle out the answers to these and many other similarly unappealing questions. Once you have understood the relatively simple relationships involved, however, it is easier to understand and appreciate the arguments for shifting this country to the metric system and putting it in line with the rest of the world.

Meters and kilometers measure distance, as do miles and yards; grams and kilograms measure weight, as do ounces and pounds. . . .

Theme A begins with an anecdote (which could have been made more effective if the man and his family had been more specifically described so that the reader could relate to them more closely), proceeds with a paragraph of facts and statistics, and then moves into the development of the thesis sentence.

Theme B relies on an unusual observation, while Theme C introduces its topic by highlighting the relevance of the point to the intended audience (the student's peer group). Theme D begins by providing some background information to the reader before launching into its argument in favor of the metric system.

Each of these themes might have been introduced in a different fashion. The student writing the first one could have depicted the scene at a card game or a race track where Joe McPherson was gambling, or she could have shown Joe trying to explain his losses to his wife. Or she could have stayed away from the anecdote introduction entirely, instead providing a brief history of the problem in the community or the country or using a quotation to start out.

The theme about microwave ovens could have begun with a brief history of their development or how they worked, with a description of how they alter the taste of food (as compared with more conventional methods of cooking), or with an anecdote about how the quick-cooking qualities of the microwave oven can be important to marital harmony when both partners work.

Theme C could have begun with an anecdote or a series of brief anecdotes focusing attention on specific problems of the elderly; it could have begun with statistics of various kinds; it could have begun with quotations such as "Grow old with me/The best is yet to be" (from Robert Browning's "Rabbi Ben Ezra"), showing how the picture painted is not the reality.

Theme D, finally, could have begun by assuming that the reader already knows the basics of the metric system. The student writer could have shown how using metrics could save time and money for businesses, or he could have used statistics to underscore the cost of changing over to the metric system (if he did that, however, he would have to argue that the cost was justified).

No matter what theme you are writing, there are always many ways to introduce it, just as there are many ways to develop and support your thesis sentence. Since the introductory paragraphs will be your reader's first impression of your theme, it is worth your while to consider them carefully and to try several approaches.

You will probably have better success with your introductions if you write them last, beginning your rough drafts with your thesis sentence as suggested. There are several advantages to this procedure, the most important of which is that you get launched immediately into the rough-draft-writing process without being sidetracked with the complexities of introducing a theme that has not yet been developed. You do not waste time introducing thesis sentences that you will discard later. Once you have developed your theme fully (including the conclusion), you are in a better position to evaluate the kind of introduction needed, perhaps using that paragraph or two to introduce some variety into the theme as well as to set up the thesis and topic sentences. And with your theme fully developed you will be unlikely to wander away from your topic into unnecessary if interesting background information.

When you are planning your introductory paragraph or paragraphs, you should consider your theme as a whole and the congeniality of your topic and thesis sentence for your audience. Short themes—themes of 400 or 500 words—should in general have short introductions to keep the proportions appropriate. If your introduction to a 500-word theme consists of 100 words or more, it is probably too long, unless you have very good reasons for that much introductory material. A longer theme can take more introduction without seeming out of shape. But you will have to use your judgment to ensure that your introduction is relevant to your thesis and your audience and that it does not usurp too much of your theme as a whole.

CONCLUDING PARAGRAPHS
Your conclusion is important because it makes the final impression on your reader. It is your last chance to make—or lose—your point.

Conclusions can summarize a theme as a whole, restate the theme's most vital argument, relate the theme to larger issues or to a reader's self-interest, or restate the thesis exactly or with some variations.

A

In conclusion, the problems of the elderly are our problems because, as people of high standards, we must care about the problems of others; because, as citizens and taxpayers, we must contribute to social security and other programs whether we want to or not, and whether they are good programs or not; because, as intelligent people, we have a responsibility to solve these problems if we can; and because, as people, we will be old some day.

B

Thus, the metric system will have a profound impact on the nature and quality of all aspects of American life, from the container of milk on your refrigerator shelf, to the tooling up of American industries.

EXERCISE 1
With the consent of your instructor, select a theme that you have written as part of an earlier assignment in this course. Revise it, focusing

your attention on paragraph length and topic sentence use and place-ment. Intersperse short paragraphs with longer ones to vary the rhythm and pace of your presentation. Vary your topic sentence placement so that some paragraphs begin with their topic sentences, some conclude with them, and some have topic sentences buried within the paragraph or in another paragraph. Underline your thesis sentence twice and your topic sentences once so that the structure of your theme is clear. Obvi-ously, you would not perform this kind of exercise with all of your themes, but it is useful to do it this time so that you develop your sense of what is possible and your skill in controlling your paragraphs.

EXERCISE 2
Again for the purpose of developing your skills, select a topic from the following list (or another topic, with the consent of your instructor). Write a paragraph consisting of reasons, one of details (you may invent facts and statistics if you wish), one of quotations, and one of compari-sons.

TOPICS
1. Old age in America
2. The greatest problem on campus
3. Famous last words
4. The strangest experience I have ever had
5. Ethics in government

EXERCISE 3
Select one of the topics from the list in exercise 2 (it may be the one you chose for that exercise) and write a letter to the editor of your campus or local newspaper or to a government agency or to a political officeholder or to another appropriate audience. Perform the rough-draft procedures necessary to limit your topic, develop your thesis and topic sentences, and gather and evaluate ideas. Then plan for para-graph variety, using the techniques you learned in this chapter. Write the letter.

After a period away from your work (preferably a day or more), re-vise it, concentrating on your paragraphs. Try to develop full and con-vincing paragraphs of varying lengths and with different types of topic sentence placement and various paragraph kinds. Concentrate too on the quality of your introductory and concluding paragraphs to make your argument or point of view as convincing as possible.

chapter 7

putting sparkle into your sentences

1. Sentence Patterns and Variety

> 1. Around the house ran the boy.
> 2. The boy ran around the house.
> 3. The boy around the house ran.
> 4. Around the boy ran the house.
> 5. The around boy house the ran.

Even a cursory glance at the samples just given reveals a number of intriguing facts about sentences and what you *already know* about acceptable sentence structure in English. For example, you recognize the first sentence as a possible if relatively unusual variation of the normal subject–verb pattern. You automatically accept the second pattern as the normal one—the most familiar, the one that requires the least attention to understand, the one you are most likely to see and use.

The third example seems to make no sense at first. Before you can understand it to mean anything, you would need to add some facts: Apparently, there is a boy lounging around the house, and he ran. Thus, you have a sentence that reads, "The boy (who was lounging) around the house ran." There is a procedure for this process in English grammar, used frequently in commands like "Go to the store!" The subject, "you," is understood in such a sentence (the technical term for this process is *ellipsis*; the sentence would be called elliptical). But since this is a rather unusual use of ellipsis, you might correctly believe that the sentence is ungrammatical and has no meaning. At the very least, it is awkward and should be rewritten.

Sentence 4 also seems like nonsense, since it is impossible in the "real world" for a house to run around a boy. Yet, the nouns notwithstanding, the structure of the sentence is correct. If you did not know that the actions were impossible, or if you were reading a fantasy in which such actions were possible, you would have no trouble understanding the *structure* of that sentence. Sentences have structures separate from their meaning, and like syllogisms, sentences can be valid (structurally correct) without being true (factually correct).

Your sentence sense tells you that the fifth example is not possible in English. Prepositions like *around* cannot modify nouns like *boy*. Articles (or adjectives, depending on your grammar book) like *the* cannot modify verbs like *ran*. The amazing thing is that you know that the sentence just does not work, whether or not you can name the parts of speech or describe the reasons. Your sentence sense tells you—just as your sentence sense tells you that example 1 is quite acceptable, example 2 is ordinary, example 3 is strange but possible, and example 4 makes sense as a structure but not as a statement of fact.

It is important that you have this confidence in yourself and in what you already know about sentences and sentence structure. For years you have been using all of the patterns you will soon read about, even though you may not now (or ever, for that matter) be able to name them correctly. It is not important that you be able to name them; it *is* important that you be able to use them. All of which is preparation for saying that you should not let complicated-sounding names distract you from the real business of practicing sentence variety. The names are tools in the discussion of kinds of sentences, no more, no less.

Like paragraphs, sentences can be very short.

Other sentences, like this one, can, through the process of inserting modifiers like adjectives and adverbs, and through the process of subordinating and coordinating clauses, become extremely long, even to the point of distracting the reader from the very meaning the writer intended to convey, no matter how precisely each word was selected and no matter how determined the reader is to pay careful attention to what has been printed on the page.

In effect, the attention span of any reader is limited. A sentence should be just long enough to convey its meaning (careful subordination and coordination included), and no longer.

A long sentence in a paragraph of short ones will stand out as important (or odd, if it is badly handled), as will a very short sentence in a group of long ones. Varying the length of your sentences will help alter the pace of your theme and thus help keep the reader attentive.

Sentences can be categorized, also, according to their structural patterns. *Simple sentences* have a single subject and a single verb, though the sentence can be of any length.

1. He ran.
2. The tall, handsome, muscular man ran quickly and fearfully around the block.

It is sometimes confusing that simple sentences may have more than one part to the subject and verb, so long as there is just the one main subject and one main verb.

3. He and she/ ran and jumped.
4. The tall, handsome, muscular man and the short, fat girl/ ran.

When two simple sentences are yoked together by a coordinating conjunction (a group including only the following words: *and, or, but, for, nor, yet, so*), it is called a *compound sentence*.

1. The boy ran *but* the girl jumped.
2. The boy and the girl ran, *yet* both were caught.
3. Sugar is sweet *and* so are you.
4. He ran *and* she jumped.

By its very structure a compound sentence indicates to the reader that the two concepts held together are of an equal level of generality or importance or pertinence.

A *complex sentence* is appropriate if one of the concepts to be discussed is less important than the other.

1. *Because* the boy ran, the girl jumped.
2. *Although* the boy and the girl ran, both were caught.
3. *If* sugar is sweet, so are you.

The first clause (*clause* is another word for simple sentence) in each of these examples is subordinated because it is introduced by a subordinating conjunction (any conjunction other than *and, or, but, for, nor, yet, so*). The subordinated clause need not come first.

4. The girl jumped *because* the boy ran.
5. Both were caught, *although* the boy and the girl ran.
6. So are you (sweet) *if* sugar is sweet.

TABLE 7
Sentences—The Structural Classes

Structural Class	Definition	Examples	Effect on Reader
Simple	A single clause; one subject and one verb in agreement with the subject, although each may be compound.	1. I love you. 2. Jane and I hate our brothers.	Basic statement; relative importance to discussion not determined by sentence structure itself.
Compound	Two or more simple sentences linked by a coordinating conjunction (*and, or, but, for, nor, yet, so*).	1. I love you but I hate Paul. 2. Jane and I hate our brothers and we love our sisters.	Two basic statements made equally important by sentence structure.
Complex	Two clauses, one of which is introduced by a subordinating conjunction (e.g., *although, if, when*—any conjunction other than the seven coordinating conjunctions).	1. When I love you, I hate Paul. 2. Jane and I hate our brothers although we love our sisters.	Statement introduced by subordinating conjunction shown to be less important than or dependent on the other (main) clause.
Compound/complex	Three or more clauses, at least one of which is dependent.	When I love you, I hate Paul and I feel miserable.	Relative importance of clauses indicated by conjunctions; placing all in the same sentence indicates that they are part of a single major idea.

But your reader will still understand the thought presented by such a clause as the lesser or dependent thought—something to keep in mind as you revise your paragraphs to heighten their precision.

Predictably, a sentence with two equal clauses (compound) and one or more subordinated clauses (complex) is called a compound–complex sentence.

1. *Although* both were happy with the arrangement, Esther was seeking something better *and* June had other things on her mind.
2. John worked hard *while* Ralph loafed *and* Rodney did his usual quota of work.

The word *although* subordinates the first clause in sentence 1; the other two are coordinated (by the conjunction *and*). The word *while* subordinates the second clause of the second example; the other two clauses are coordinate.

Simple, compound, complex, and compound–complex are categories that separate sentences by their structure. (See Table 7.) But sentences can also be classified by their function in the paragraph.

A *declarative* sentence makes a statement; it is the most common kind of sentence. An *interrogative* sentence asks a question; an *imperative* sentence gives a command; an *exclamatory* sentence (or sentence fragment) expresses strong emotion. Each kind of sentence will have a different effect on the reader and require various amounts of reader involvement. (See Table 8.)

TABLE 8
Sentences—By Function

Example	*Kind*	*Effect*
1. The door is closed.	Declarative (statement)	Reader is neutral.
2. Is the door closed?	Interrogative (question)	Reader is forced to look (or consider), judge, and report on findings.
3. Close the door!	Imperative (command)	Reader is forced to act.
4. My god, the door is closed!	Exclamatory (emotion)	Reader wonder why this matters so sympathizes, or whatever is appropriate.

English offers you other sentence patterns as well, most of which you already use in your everyday conversations. For example, you may begin your sentences with prepositional phrases, gerunds, adverbs, and other parts of speech (and do so every day, even if you cannot identify which is which), and you can move adverbs around in your sentences to achieve different effects. (See Table 9.)

TABLE 9
Various Sentence Patterns

Example	*Kind*	*Effect*
1. The children ran *into the* rain.	Prepositional phrase	1. Ordinary position.
2. *Into the rain* ran the children.		2. Sentence inverted, unusual, striking.
3. John and Mary danced happily together and they won the contest.	Compound sentence	3. Satisfactory, but subordination would help.
4. Dancing happily together, John and Mary won the contest.	Participial phrase	4. Variety; helps relate ideas and show importance.
5. He ran quickly.	Subject–verb–adverb	5. Normal pattern.
6. Quickly he ran.	Adverb first	6. Less common; not unusual.
7. He quickly ran.	Adverb embedded	7. Unusual in this position, but correct; calls attention to sentence.

English also gives you the choice between using *loose* or *periodic* sentences. Loose sentences get the main idea across in the first clause, adding modifiers such as prepositional phrases or subordinated clauses at the end. Such sentences convey the main idea immediately; most English sentences function in this fashion. Periodic sentences, on the other hand, embed modifiers inside the first clause, making the reader wait much longer for the main idea to be completed. If properly handled, periodic sentences can hold the reader in suspense; if handled poorly, they will confuse the reader instead.

LOOSE: The boy kissed the girl, who was quite beautiful, charming, scintillating, and downright appealing.

PERIODIC: The boy kissed the beautiful, charming, and downright appealing pet frog.

As you revise your themes, you will want to consider the kinds of sentences available to you to express your meanings precisely and to achieve specific effects for your reader. You do not do this work as part of your rough draft (in most cases) because it slows you down in your attempt to capture your major ideas and build your framework and because it makes little sense to polish sentences that you may later have to discard. And even as you revise you will want to give first priority to the clarity and precision with which your ideas are expressed—long and complicated sentences are not your goal now any more than they were earlier. But you do want to use subordination and variety to help express the logical meaning of your ideas.

1. The politician took the bribe and he went on about his business.
2. The politician went on about his business although he had just taken the bribe.
3. Although he had just taken the bribe, the politician went on about his business.

You can see that each of these sentences expresses a different version of the idea. In the first one, the two concepts are equal (that is, it is a compound sentence). In the second and third, the concept of taking the bribe has been subordinated by the subordinating conjunction *although* (that is, they are complex sentences). The second sentence is loose (major clause first, modifying concepts later). You find out about the bribe only after having completed the whole sentence. On the other hand, your opinion is formed much earlier in the third example; you know about the bribe before the politician is mentioned. You sense that these ideas, while similar, are not identical, and you react accordingly as a reader. As a writer, you attempt to control the impact on the reader through the skill with which you select sentence patterns to express your ideas precisely.

It may be helpful at this point to look at several student themes to see how rough drafts can be revised with attention to the precision and variety of the sentences.

A: Rough Draft

Apples and Alligators

My greatest problem in choosing a career is that I am interested in so many kinds of things.

I am interested in apples. I want to know about the varieties and how they are grown and harvested. And I am interested in alligators. I want to know all about them; I want to know such useful things as how many teeth they have and how you can tell the difference between an alligator and a crocodile.

The same variety of interests holds true in careers. I am interested in science, enough to be a doctor or perhaps a chemist. But I am also interested in literature. I love to read and would enjoy a career which allowed me to do so. And I am interested in politics and philosophy and history.

My problem is that I have not yet been able to select from my many interests to focus my attention along a career path. I hope to do so soon since such a decision will be necessary in order to focus on a major field of study in college.

A: Revised

Apples and Alligators

If you've ever been a crazy young kid, boy or girl doesn't matter in this case, you know how it is to wonder about the world. Why are there stars at night and not during the day? Where does the sun *really* go at night? What makes a plane stay in the air? Why is an apple red or green and not orange or yellow? How many teeth does an alligator have? If an alligator battled a crocodile, which would win?

Part of the joy of my life is that somehow, in spite of the urge to conform with the world, I have been able to maintain this great fascination with life. Everything holds my attention: science and literature, politics and art and philosophy and history. But that is also part of my problem now that I must focus on a field of study for a career.

Apples and alligators aside, I must be able to put some order into my life, to pick and choose among the various tempting alternatives, and to select what is most important to me. It is to this task that I now turn my attention.

B: Rough Draft

Choosing a Career

It was easy for me to select a career since I always wanted to be an actress. That wish goes back almost as far as I can remember.

In order to attain my career goal, I am studying theater arts and drama with a minor in business administration. The minor is because I am a realistic person. I know that I might not make it as an actress, or I might not make it right away. The business is so I don't starve along the route. It also will help me to manage my money, assuming I make any in my acting career.

B: Revised

Choosing a Career

If you've ever wondered what Lady Macbeth, Peter Pan, and the Wizard of Oz have in common, the answer is me. At one time or another I have *been* all of these people—and more.

I have always wanted to be an actress, ever since I was a small child and realized the power of a pout or a smile over the adults who determined my life. Thus, in a sense, I have always been "studying" acting. Now at college I am majoring in theater arts and drama.

But I have always been a realist too, which is the reason for my minor in business administration. I figure that if worst comes to worst, I can always support myself. And if the best materializes, I will know how to manage my money.

C: Rough Draft

Not "Roto-Rooter," but . . .

This is not going to be your ordinary type theme about "what I want to be when I grow up." I am already grown up, and have been for some years. I am not here to "find myself" or to "choose my course in life." That has already been chosen. By profession, I am a plumber. Not a famous one or even a rich one, though I am not starving certainly. I am at college to improve myself as a person. So this theme assignment is not really relevant to me.

C: Revision

Not "Roto-Rooter," but . . .

My outlook on a "career choice" is different, probably, from most of the other people in this class since I am much older than most of them. I have been in the army and my children are, or in the case of my youngest son, will be teenagers. My career choice was made many years ago, and not entirely of my "free will."

I did not have the luxury of deciding what to "be" after exploring the various academic disciplines. I had to get a job and earn a living. I became a plumber since it was the first job with a future (monetary) available to me. Sometimes things happen that way.

And I could tell you plumbing tales. But this is not the time or place for that. Instead, I will just say that being a plumber is a totally nonglamorous but respectable operation. You go into a lot of places which are not so nice, and you meet all kinds of people. And all of them need you *right away.* In that sense, being a plumber is like being a doctor.

This class means something else to me other than a vehicle for choosing a career. I am here, though it sounds trite to say it, "to get an education." I am here because I want to be. And because of that, I will learn more.

As you read the rough drafts and the revisions of these student themes, you probably noticed some striking differences. For one thing, not just the sentences were changed. New ideas were added; details were deleted, and in the third theme at least, the concept of the conclusion was substantially changed to make the theme "do the assignment" rather than complain about it. (The complaint may well have been justified, but it did not belong in the theme itself.) No revision changes just the sentences, though attention to sentence structure and precision is an important element of the revision process.

Let us consider the "Apples and Alligators" theme first.

The rough draft of that theme is an adequate treatment of the assignment for a rough draft. It selects a thesis sentence idea ("My greatest problem in choosing a career is that I am interested in so many kinds of things") and stays with it, showing how it holds true in a career choice as it had previously in other things. Using the "apples and alligators" analogy helps bring the rough draft to life, although it could be misleading as a title. A person looking at that title is likely to be intrigued enough by it to start reading the theme but at the same time to have absolutely no idea what the theme subject was. A title should both inform and intrigue.

The revision adds precise details in the first paragraph to help the reader relate to the experience; the student uses an interrogative sentence pattern to pull the reader into the theme. Her initial sentence now is one with which any reader can have some sympathy ("If *you've* ever been a crazy young kid, *boy or girl doesn't matter* in this case . . .") rather than a statement of her problem, which may or may not interest the reader. The theme concludes with a much stronger statement of purpose than the one made in the rough draft.

Your own analysis of the second and third themes will reveal how questions, new and less usual sentence patterns, and the addition of details help strengthen the presentations. As you revise your own themes now, you will want to concentrate your attention on just such matters so that the very structure of each sentence you write contributes effectively to the overall thrust of your theme.

EXERCISE 1

Compare the rough draft of theme B with its revision. How does the revision improve the original? In what ways, if any, was the original better? Do the same for theme C. Be prepared to defend your conclusions in class.

EXERCISE 2

Select a student theme from a chapter in Unit One of this book. Analyze it in terms of what you now know about revision. Where does it fall short? Rewrite the theme, concentrating on developing more effective paragraphs and using a variety of sentence patterns to enhance the presentation. If you prefer, you may select one of the themes you have written for an earlier assignment in this course and revise that instead.

EXERCISE 3

How does this course (or other courses you are now taking) relate to your future career? Prepare a rough draft for a 500- to 750-word theme on this topic (or another topic, with the consent of your instructor). Then revise your theme, concentrating on paragraphs and sentences. Turn in your rough draft and your revision. Be prepared to discuss the difference between the two in class.

EXERCISE 4

Select a short newspaper article or editorial on a topic that is current. What kinds of paragraphs and sentences does your article or editorial use? Select an article or editorial on the same topic in a news magazine. Are the styles the same? If not, in what ways are they different? Be prepared to discuss your conclusions in class.

EXERCISE 5

Select at least four of the following writers and read a short essay, poem, or passage in a book by each in order to get some sense of the variety of sentences available to you. Be prepared to discuss your findings in class.

Robert Frost
John Donne
William Shakespeare
William Faulkner
William Butler Yeats
James Baldwin
William Buckley
John F. Kennedy
George Elliot

2. Sentence Rhythms

Rhythms—the pushing and pulling, the swaying and shoving, the way the very structure of your sentences propels you through them—now it is time to stop and listen, to feel the pulse of what you have written and learn to control the impetus of your prose.

Consider the following sentences, analyzing them to see how they move you through their meanings:

1. I went home for Christmas. I didn't want to go.
2. Although I really didn't want to go and although I fought valiantly against the prospect, I in fact went home for Christmas.
3. I, being of less than sound mind around holidays, went, I hesitate to tell you where for fear that, with everything else you know about me, you would think me mad or at the very least inconsistent, home—for Christmas.
4. It was for Christmas that I went home.

Each way of expressing the idea has a different impact, caused in part by the patterns of subordination and coordination, in part by the order of presentation, and in part by the rhythm of the sentence—all working together to create a single effect on you as the reader. Here is where you use what you've learned about sentence structure and variety as you write. Let's look at each of the sample sentences, using arrows and slashes to try to indicate how it works in terms of its pushes and pulls. (The arrows and slashes have no meaning aside from this, and other symbols might have been used instead to function as stops or pushers in this discussion.)

I went home for Christmas. I didn't want to go.

Sample 1 consists of two simple sentences. Although you may sense the rhythms of the subunits in several ways depending on your own speech patterns, you probably sense no urgency in the structure. You are not propelled through the meaning but walk through it one word at a time, on your own, as if you were moving across a level platform.

I/ went/ home for Christmas.]I/didn't/want to go.]

In sample 2, on the other hand, your motion is controlled by the subordinated pattern that initiates it, by the fact that the completion of the sentence is put off twice by the subordinated pattern (*although* is repeated), and by the nature of its details. The subordination and the details hold the meaning away from you but push you forward, making you read faster to learn what will happen. This kind of sentence structure makes you feel as if you are moving at an uneven pace up and down hills of meaning:

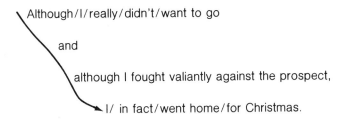

Although/I/really/didn't/want to go

and

although I fought valiantly against the prospect,

I/ in fact/went home/for Christmas.

Again, the exact pacing will depend on your speech rhythms, but the ultimate impact of this sentence is to push you through its meaning, and perhaps to let you down at its conclusion. Why, you wonder, is going home for Christmas worth the valiant struggle? The context (the surrounding material) of the theme would have to provide that information.

Sample 3 keeps stopping you:

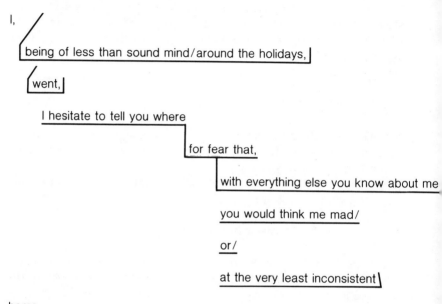

It lives in an odd, mad structure of subordination within subordination, a special effect, not often found in formal writing outside fiction or poetry.

Sample 4 is far more ordinary, turning its meaning around in its structure to hold the reader off for a little while:

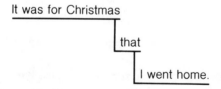

This sentence seems to be the strangely phrased answer to the question; Why did you go home? "It was for Christmas that I went home." The structure is odd, though, and does not disappear into the meaning of the sentence as it would, say, had the answer been "I went home for Christmas."

You may not have the time—or the inclination—to go far enough into the revising process to enjoy the sentence rhythms for each of your themes or to control them so that they have the impact you want on your reader. Yet they are not something that you should automatically overlook. It is certainly true that the rhythmic patterns of your sentences can help you hurry your reader through a part of your discussion that will be unpleasant, or make your reader stop and consider. There is an almost infinite variety of rhythms and ways of expressing yourself that are yours for the using, and they are fun to experiment with. And there is no "right" way.

Each of the sample sentences is a legitimate expression of an idea in an acceptable English sentence structure. What is "right" depends on what works best in the context of the theme and the writer's purpose. Sentence rhythms are a communication tool well worth exploring for the impact they have on your reader, for the verve they add to your style, and for the pleasure they add to the writing process.

EXERCISE 1
Develop at least five versions of the following sentences, using sentence structure and rhythm to vary their meaning and impact. Be prepared to analyze the various changes and how they affect you. For what writing situation would each be most suitable?

1. Down the stairs ran the child.
2. In spite of the fact that I was very happy, I left school and went home.
3. Candy is dandy.
4. Sex appeal may be defined as one of the characteristics most important in young men and women—at least according to television commercials.

EXERCISE 2
Select one of the student themes in this book or one of your own and rewrite it, concentrating on sentence rhythms and structure to fine-tune the meaning of what you have to say and its impact on your reader.

EXERCISE 3

Pay some attention to the kinds of sentence patterns and rhythms you use in your speech. Most of us employ a great variety of patterns in a natural situation, such as a friendly conversation, but have difficulty incorporating those patterns into the more formal situation of writing. If you have trouble listening to yourself in this fashion, listen to your friends, family, instructors, or television personalities. Try, as you write, to use some of the patterns that come easily to you when you are speaking.

EXERCISE 4

Select several of the magazines that you read on a regular basis (if you don't have regular magazine-reading habits, select a woman's magazine, a sports magazine, and a business magazine). Examine each for the kinds and lengths of paragraphs used. Is the magazine consistent, or does the style of the story seem to depend on the content and author? Can you make any statements about the length and rhythm of the sentences and how they move you through the stories? Does each magazine set a style that you can describe? How might the style, if there is one, relate to the audience for the magazine as well as its subject matter? Be prepared to discuss your conclusions in class.

3. Sentence Problems

In many public schools across the country, discussions of "grammar" are no longer common. An effective discussion of "grammar" never was.

You learned most of the grammar you will ever need to know to write in an educated fashion when you were a small child learning to speak. A few confusing moments aside, it is a fact that you recognize sentences and nonsentences without having to stop to analyze them. Usually, in the "real world," the confusing moments don't matter because almost everyone is confused by the same few grammatical choices: Is it "Whom may I say is calling?" or is it "Who may I say is calling?"

School grammar, if you learned it at all, probably taught you to label. You could recognize a noun and pick out a conjunctive adverb, all of which will be important to you if you decide to go on with your study of writing. That is because having agreed-upon labels for parts of speech helps people discuss their use and function. In the same way you will probably learn to label the various kinds of sentences. For now, however, we will pay attention to the sentence problems that cause confusion in meaning and to those that are so "wrong" that other educated people would not use them in formal writing situations. If you make the kinds of mistakes discussed in this section, ask your instructor to recommend a grammar book to you so that you can learn the appropriate rules.

But your sentence problems will generally occur not because you need to learn rules but because you have written in a hurry and have not devoted sufficient energy to revising. Your modifiers may be placed in the wrong part of your sentences; your subjects may not agree with your verbs; your pronouns may shift or suffer because their meanings are unclear in context, and you may use a passive construction because it was the first thing that came to mind, rather than being precise enough to state your meaning clearly. (See Table 10.)

TABLE 10

Example	Problem	Correction/Comments
1. The dog caught the ball with the big bark.	Misplaced modifier	1. The dog with the big bark caught the ball.
2. The politician was chided by the man who took the bribe.	Misplaced modifier?	2. The politician who took the bribe was chided by the man.
3. Paul and John fought before he was killed.	Unclear pronoun reference	3. Paul and John fought before Paul (or John or Bob) was killed.
4. The box of candies are on the table.	Subject-verb agreement.	4. The *box* of candies *is* on the table.
5. To dance and singing are my favorite things to do.	Incorrect parallel structure.	5. Dancing and singing (or to dance and to sing) are my favorite things to do.
6. It happened yesterday when she comes home.	Verb tenses wrong	6. It happened yesterday when she came home.
7. Because I want to.	Fragment	7. I do it because I want to. Fragments are acceptable in some writing situations; ask your instructor.
8. She works hard and she wins	Subordination	8. She wins because she works hard (or, She works hard because she wins). Sentence improved by clarifying relationship of ideas.
9. It was done too quickly.	Weak passive	9. I did it too quickly.

By now you are probably aware of the kinds of sentence problems that recur in your themes. As you are revising you will want to focus your attention on these to eliminate them from your writing once and for all.

EXERCISE 1
Read the following student paragraphs to determine what kinds of sentence problems they contain. Be prepared to discuss your conclusions in class. After you have diagnosed the problems, revise the paragraphs so that they are acceptable.

A

Rush hour can be eliminated with a little thought. Since everyone really does not have to go to work at the same time. It seemed to me that we will have to do something very soon before everyone goes crazy.

B

I think that I have to work too hard to succeed in life. Each day, I have to go to school, selling sodas at the shopping center fountain, and do the normal daily chores of cleaning house and other things like that. It is too bad that when I am young, I have not been able to spend time enjoying myself as I should.

C

"Everyone does it, so why shouldn't I?" A phrase often heard by parents of every generation and one which is very hard to answer. As a parent myself, my response is that if everyone does it, they shouldn't be doing it. So I tell my kids not to. Not to just follow the crowd blindly. If they want to do something let them bring me good reasons why. Then I may reconsider.

EXERCISE 2
If you have a particular sentence problem or group of problems, spend an hour or two reviewing a grammar book to help resolve them. Prepare a chart like the one in this chapter, including an example of the specific kind of problem sentence, the relevant rule, and the problem sentence, properly corrected.

chapter 8

selecting exactly the right word

1. Denotation and Connotation

Even the very words that make up your sentences are worthy of your attention as part of the revision process. Communication, after all, is made up of words—words held together in predictable ways, to be sure, but words nonetheless.

As the units of thought and communication, the words you select to convey your meaning to your readers will "mean" to your readers on many levels. Words have the kind of meaning called *denotation*. The denotation or *sign* of a word is the definition you might find in the dictionary. If you understand the denotation of a word and I understand it, we both understand pretty much the same thing. The word *Stop* printed on a stop sign means "Bring your vehicle to a halt" to all who "understand" that word.

Words also have the kind of meaning called *connotation* or *symbolism*. These are the overtones of words, the differences in feeling and degree that each of us brings from our past experience into conversations and communications in the present. While you and I share the denotative meaning of the word *mother*, our connotative interpretations of that word are likely to be quite different. The same is true for most of the emotionally charged words about which people talk and argue, words like *patriotism* and *freedom* and *rights*. Before any real communication can occur, people must agree on what these words "mean" in the discussion context. Otherwise, people will continue to argue "at" each other, with little real communication in evidence.

Consider the following student theme:

A

Academic Freedom

The schools and universities of this nation are the repositories of a very previous commodity and one which is well worth protecting. I am talking about freedom, academic freedom.

Academic freedom is one of the most vital aspects of any university. It allows faculty to achieve their greatest capacity and trains students in the valuable lessons of American tradition. Academic freedom is truly worth protecting against all encroachments, from outside the university or inside.

With your experience in selecting and limiting topics, you probably have determined the problem with this student theme. It is too general and vague, never getting into the topic. Themes that deal with highly connotative words like *freedom* tend to suffer from this malady. Connotative or symbolic words are hard to define—it is difficult to say exactly what they mean, and so it is tempting to talk around them. Forcing yourself to be specific will help remedy the problem. Here is how another student handled the topic of "academic freedom."

B

Academic Freedom

Through the years, academic freedom has been the subject of much discussion and the rallying point for many battles. But these are the subjects for history books, not themes.

For me, academic freedom means the right to explore ideas and to formulate my own opinions, irrespective of the opinions expressed by my professors. I will listen respectfully to the political judgments of my poli sci instructors and to the philosophical musings of the instructor in Philosophy

100. But I will not take the next step with them. I will not agree with them (if I don't) in class or on exams just in order to get a good grade. To do so is to make a mockery not only of my academic freedom but of the very purpose of a college education, which must be to develop your own ability to think and reason and to come to sound conclusions.

The second student recognized that she had a topic that had to be limited in order to be handled properly. While it is still a rough draft, her theme is far more successful than the first one because she reduced the level of generality at which the discussion of this difficult, connotative topic takes place. In other words, rather than discussing *the concept* of academic freedom she discussed *her concept* of academic freedom. We come away from the theme with a sense of the person who wrote it and her integrity, as well as with an understanding of "academic freedom" itself.

It will be helpful to your reader if, as you handle the highly connotative, emotionally charged concepts you will face in your college and real-life writing experiences, you remember to be specific, to provide examples of what you mean, and to reduce the level of generality of the discussion where possible. Sometimes the task is simple, a matter of citing a specific instance rather than a conclusion. For example, rather than saying "Alan is a patriot" you might say "Alan risked his life for his country." The second statement conveys more meaning than the first because it is more precise. Other times you might have to provide your reader with your definition (denotative if appropriate, as well as connotative) for the word so that no confusion results.

C

Jerome Walter—Patriot

I realize that under some definitions of the word, my uncle Jerome's actions would be considered anything but "patriotic." Instead of fighting in Vietnam, he fled to Canada, and there made a new life for himself, a life which included a wife, a responsible job, and a family.

But he did not leave America because he was a coward, afraid to die. Nor was it because it was against his moral beliefs to kill for his country.

Jerome says, and I believe him, that he would be willing to fight and die for his country and to kill for it if necessary. He did not fight in Vietnam because he did not consider that war to be in the best interests of this country or that one. America had nothing to gain and everything to lose, the politicians' rhetoric notwithstanding. From my point of view, his actions make him just as much a patriot as those men who went to war because they believed it to be in America's best interest for them to do so. Unfortunately, the label of "coward" will probably remain his for the rest of his life.

After reading this theme, you may agree or disagree with the writer's perception of Jerome Walter as a "patriot." But you *understand* what the writer meant by the use of the word. A patriot, to this writer, is someone who will do anything that is in the "best interests of the country," no matter what the risks are, but, again according to this writer, a patriot does not have to follow blindly where leaders point.

EXERCISE 1
Select one of the following topics and write a 500- to 750-word theme, remembering to limit your topic and to reduce the generality of discussion where appropriate. Use specific examples to illustrate your points, and vary your paragraphs and sentence rhythms.

TOPICS
1. Democracy
2. Patriotism
3. Liberty
4. Law and the United States
5. Equality
6. Sexual freedom

If you prefer, you may try to prepare a brief article for your campus newspaper or for one of the magazines you have examined in a previous exercise. If the newspaper or magazine you select seems to have a specific style, try to use that in your discussion.

EXERCISE 2
Choose three of the following words; consult reference sources, including the *Oxford English Dictionary*, a speakers' handbook, a dictionary of quotations, and others, to define them. Write a paragraph or two defining each; deal with denotative as well as connotative meanings.

1. Friendship
2. Love
3. Success

4. Health
5. Failure
6. Money
7. Education
8. Life

EXERCISE 3
Select three of the words you did not use in exercise 2. For each of these, develop a sequence of specific subcategories that might include specific examples of events in your own life. For example:

Knowledge ⟶ Written knowledge ⟶ Libraries ⟶

Books ⟶ Books in English ⟶ Fiction ⟶

Mystery fiction ⟶ Perry Mason books ⟶

My favorite Perry Mason book.

How does specifying the topic change it? How does it clarify it? What is lost? Be prepared to discuss your findings in class.

2. Figures of Speech

Figures of speech are linguistic tools that poets and fiction writers and essayists and other "professionals" often use to enrich the style of their work and to bring their ideas to life for their readers. You are now at the stage in your writing career where you too can employ these communication tools to convey your meanings to your readers.

The figures of speech available to you include simile and metaphor, irony, understatement and overstatement and personification. Another highly useful and less well-known figure of speech is *litotes*.

A *simile* is a comparison that used the word *like* or *as*. A *metaphor* is a comparison that does not use either of those two words:

SIMILE: She is as lovely as a rose.
She is like a rose.

METAPHOR: She is a rose.

The effect of a metaphor is to equate two ideas; the effect of a simile is to point up similarities.

You are using *irony* when you say one thing and mean something else, usually the opposite of the denotative meaning of what you have just said. Irony can be a matter of the tone of your voice in spoken conversation (as in "You are a *real* friend," said to someone who has just betrayed you) or the tone within the context of a written piece.

For example, you would be using irony if you wrote a theme about how "pleasant" exercise is when all the examples show that you really hate it. You would be using irony if you wrote an essay calling a politician a "true servant of the people" when the facts you describe prove that the opposite is true. And you would be using irony if you described an annual inflation rate of 22 percent as "low" or "relatively low."

A

The Future of These United States

I am optimistic about the future of these United States. What else could I be when this country seems to be approaching the relatively low annual inflation rate of 22 percent—22.23 percent to be exact.

It is fortunate for us that, as most people don't realize, inflation is actually geometric in its impact rather than linear. What I mean is this. Suppose there is an "annual inflation rate" of 7 percent. That means that the cost of, for example, shipping a widget from here to there is likely to go up 7 percent during a given year. And the cost of storing it is likely to go up 7 percent. And the cost of selling it—7 percent, and so on.

Now, suppose that you need to buy a widget. You get to pay the additional 7 percent to make it, ship it, store it, and sell it. Before too long, your widget would have doubled in price.

But, fortunately, that does not happen. Not in these United States.

What does happen is that the high cost of things means that some folks fortunately cannot afford to buy them. When no one can afford widgets, someone somewhere along the line must take a cut in profit or must go out of business. That drives the cost of widgets down a mite—which is how we get to the relatively low annual inflation rate of 22 percent. This country's ability to keep inflation within reasonable limits in this fashion is one of its great strengths and one of the reasons it is still a free and vigorous society.

The writer of this theme obviously does not expect the reader to take what has been written "literally" but wants him or her to share the "joke" and thus come to a more poignant realization of the problem at hand.

Understatement and *overstatement* (also called *hyperbole*) are just what their names imply. You are using understatement when you describe a situation or event as less than it is, when you call a feast "a bite to eat," for instance, or when you describe a monumental task as "a bit of a challenge." You are using overstatement when you deliberately exaggerate a situation to highlight it or to hold it up to ridicule or for some other purpose (this is very different from the accidental exaggeration that can creep into a carelessly phrased thesis sentence). Of the two, overstatement is probably easier to use, but understatement, when used well, can be more effective.

B

Cafeteria Eating

You haven't lived until you've eaten at the cafeteria. And if you do eat there, you may not live much longer.

Our cafeteria has a lot of rules, none of which is designed to improve the food or the safety of the occupants. For example, the manager wants the food to be fresh. If it has been hit by a truck within the last two weeks, it is fresh enough. And he wants the food clean. If it has ever been rained on, that is clean enough.

The other day, we had bean and bacon dripping soup. The beans were left over from the previous day's "franks and beans," which in turn had been left over from the previous Thursday's franks and beans special. The bacon drippings were not left over from anything. They were a special purchase. The manager, you understand, has pull at the supermarket. He gets bacon drippings at a cut rate.

The kindest thing I can say about the cafeteria food is that it makes your mother-in-law's cooking taste great. Nothing more could be said by mortal man.

C

Cafeteria Eating

Cafeteria eating will provide you with reasonably nutritious food at a reasonable price. Let me begin by telling you about breakfast, and you can judge the rest of the day for yourself.

For breakfast, if you choose to get up and dress and eat by 8:15 A.M., when the breakfast meal is over, you may select scrambled eggs or oatmeal for your main course. I once asked for French toast, but the cook claimed she did not know how to make it. She was telling the truth.

Anyhow, I don't much care for oatmeal, so I usually order the eggs. When they arrive, I select the least burned piece of toast, and pour myself a cup of coffee, take eight or ten napkins, and find a place to sit down. The last part is not hard, since most folks don't come to breakfast.

Three of the napkins I place on top of the eggs. I gently turn the plate over, which has the effect of putting the eggs on top of the napkins, which is what I had intended. Then I wipe the grease off of the plate with two of the clean napkins and replace the eggs. The whole process works very nicely, and with some practice, can be done in less than a minute, which means that your eggs are slightly cooler than room temperature when you finally do get to eat them. But then they say that hot food is bad for the digestion.

The difference between the exaggerated approach and the understated one is largely a matter of the writer's perspective. When you are angry, it is far easier to exaggerate ("I told you *a million times* not to slam the door") than to remain calm and understate your position.

When you use *personification*, you attribute human qualities to inanimate objects or to animals. Some personifications have become normal parts of everyday language: The wind "howls"; dogs "cry." Others give you latitude for imaginative expression.

D

Getting What You're After

The house itself seemed to hold its breath on that cold night in December when I, romanticist that I was, dragged the recalcitrant ladder inevitably towards the second floor window behind which waited Mary Diane, my fiancée. We were going to elope (a stupid idea in retrospect) and we were going to do it the *right* way (even dumber) which meant sneaking out in the middle of the night.

Halfway to the house I heard a sound and stopped. What was it? A neighborhood dog crying out the alarm? An owl (an owl???)? A burglar out to steal my marriage money? The sound of my own heart beating? The sound was gone before I could determine what it was and so, bravely I took the next step forward when something reached out and ensnared me. I fought valiantly but to no avail. The garden hose, in concert with the ladder, was more than a match for my miserable athletic skills and down I went just as a police squad car prowled by.

By the time I had explained it all to the nice officers, Mary Diane's parents had been alerted (darn it all) and the surprise elopement was spoiled. But, determined as I am, I got what I wanted—we have since been married. Unfortunately, though, I had to promise Mary Diane that we would "elope" on our first anniversary, which is why I am now looking for an apartment on the first floor.

Personification—bringing the house and the ladder and the garden hose to life—adds an atmosphere of suspense to this student essay, making it something out of the ordinary. Like all figures of speech, this one helps you select the specific descriptive details that most aptly convey the sense of the situation to the reader.

Litotes will be more useful to you in an argumentative situation. It is a way of insulting somebody without quite seeming to do so. To use it, you need simply pick a negative adjective (such as *dishonest* or *unfair* or *unkind*) and negate it with the word *not*:

LITOTES: Mr. Jamison is not an untruthful person.
That is not an unintelligent statement.

The effect of a litotes is to call the positive attribute (truth and intelligence) into doubt without making a direct attack. If, after all, Mr. Jamison were a truthful person, why say that he is "not untruthful"? If the statement were intelligent, why not simply say so?

As you begin to refine your themes, you will want to use figures of speech to highlight central arguments and to set the mood and develop the atmosphere you want. They will be assets in your attempt to gain and hold the favorable attention of your readers.

EXERCISE 1
Select three of the figures of speech described in this unit and write a brief paragraph that employs each. Try to use several examples of the figures you have selected in your paragraphs.

EXERCISE 2
Think of something in your life that irritates you. Write a three-paragraph essay (300 to 400 words) that explains it in terms of hyperbole. Then write another essay on the same topic (again, 300 to 400 words) using understatement. Which technique was more effective in this specific case? Why?

EXERCISE 3

Examine some of the great and well-known speeches by American statesmen such as Patrick Henry, Abraham Lincoln, and John Kennedy. How did figures of speech help to make their ideas memorable? How did they use unusual sentence patterns to help impress their ideas on the public mind?

3. Making Yourself Clear

In the long run making yourself clear as a writer and as a communicator is a twofold job. First, it is a matter of understanding what you want to say fully and completely enough so that you are able to select the precise words to convey your meaning. As you do this you may need to spend some time using a dictionary or a thesaurus or both to select the word with exactly the shade of meaning to suit your intent. But under most conditions you already know the precise word you need and must only make the effort to think of it. You know, for example, that a beach ball is not a *circle*, since circles are two-dimensional, but a *sphere*. The word *circle* probably comes more easily to mind, though, and if you did not stop to think, you might be tempted to use the easy but inexact description.

Second, being a communicator is a matter of understanding your audience, of gauging and evaluating the perspective of another person or persons. Words, after all, represent not only things themselves but the ways we look at things and the kinds of meanings we want to place on them. The variations in the connotative interpretations of words are but one example of this. Examples abound in real-life situations as well.

A restaurant owner, for example, looks at a cut of meat and labels it a "ham steak." The patron looks at the same cut of meat and calls it a "ham slice." Between the words *steak* and *slice* live differences in what you eat, the amount you pay, and the perspectives of the various parties. And who is "right" depends on many things, including common understanding of what the words mean, the type of restaurant in question, and so on.

Words are ways people have of manipulating experience. One reporter views something that has happened and calls it a "problem." Problems may find their place in the "B" section of the newspaper. A second reporter sees the same incident and labels it a "crisis." As a crisis, the story may belong on page 1. Recent experience has shown us that problems treated as crises can "in fact" escalate into them. So what things are called affects what they "are."

Thus, words are flexible, bending and stretching to fit what we want them to mean, being altered whether we want them to be or not by the perspectives and attitudes of the reader. Your job as a writer if you really want to communicate is to express your ideas in enough detail and with enough precision so that your reader will experience the same meaning as you do, or a meaning as close to that one as possible. It is not, for the purposes of genuine communication, sufficient to call an incident a "problem" or a "crisis." You must describe what happened so that the reader can envision it. Everything you've learned about limiting your topic and developing your theme and varying your paragraphs and controlling your sentences has been pointed toward that goal. So too is your consideration of the words in which you express your ideas.

As you revise your themes, you will want to, first of all, consider your words in terms of their literal or denotative meanings, remembering that your reader cannot ask you questions and that you as a writer have no way of evaluating your reader's state of mind or level of understanding. The more *meaning* that you can pack into your words, the better. A "nice" dress does not tell the reader as much about the scene as an "elegant" dress or a "tattered" dress or a "misshapen" dress. The more descriptive adjectives are already part of your vocabulary, though they might not come so easily to mind as words like *nice* or *pretty* or *fine*.

And as you place the final, polishing touches on your themes you will be substituting precision and control for the flexibility and interaction of speech. Since you cannot personally interact with your reader, you will have to anticipate problems and reactions. As a writer, you will need to remember that what words mean to you depends on who you are; on your family; on your neighborhood; on your interests, career, and outlook on life; and even on the mood you are in when you use them. In the real world a large part of your writing job will be to consider the perspectives of your readers: What will these words mean to these readers? How will what *they* already know and don't know color and shape their understanding of your topic? Making yourself clear ultimately means making yourself *clear to somebody* or somebodies. All of which is not to say that you should lose your own perspective or that you should abandon it to please potential readers. Rather, you will need to use all the skills you have developed in your study of writing to build bridges of understanding so that your readers may follow you easily and willingly into your way of thinking. For to bring people to you, you must begin where they are.

EXERCISE 1

Assume that you are a real-estate salesperson and that there is a parcel of land for sale in the country not far from your office. You have just listed it as your property to sell.

You have made appointments to show the land to a farmer, another real-estate broker, a zoning commissioner, an investor, an artist, the manager of an industrial park, and a naturalist. These people would be looking at the land from different perspectives, and this would color what they see, the questions they are likely to ask, and the responses that would be most likely to convince them to purchase the property. Using a table like Table 11, determine what the perspective of each of these people has to do with the presentation you would make; be prepared to discuss your conclusions and your reasons for them in class.

TABLE 11

Person	Perspective	Pitch	Reasons
Farmer			
Broker			
Commissioner			
Investor			
Artist			
Manager			
Naturalist			

EXERCISE 2

Sometimes the "meaning" of an essay or a treaty or a poem focuses on a single word or group of words. Read Robert Frost's poem, "Rose Pogonias." How does the poem pivot on the word *confused* in the last line? Be prepared to discuss your conclusions in class.

EXERCISE 3

Unlike most class writing assignments, in which the audience is the instructor and no one else, "real-world" writing tasks force you to cope with audiences of varying degrees of ability, with different amounts of interest in your topic, and with a great range of authority to solve your problem or ignore it. Thus, you must pick and choose your content as well as your style to suit whatever audience you must reach.

Select assignment A, B, C, or D. Be sure to do all parts of whichever assignment you choose. Limiting your topic carefully will help keep the amount of work you must do within reasonable bounds.

A

Memo/Work: Write a memo of 50 to 75 words explaining to a *general audience* some aspect of your job or some problem at work or a suggestion for improving working conditions. Rewrite the memo, selecting details and language to make it appropriate for your equals at work, your immediate supervisor, your immediate subordinate, the head of your company, and someone with a third-grade education.

Be prepared to explain the differences among the six memos and your reasons for them in class, or to do so in an essay written in class.

B

Apartment/Complaint: Write a letter of 50 to 75 words to a *general audience* explaining some problem that affects the tenants in your apartment complex. Rewrite the letter, selecting details and language to make it appropriate for the resident manager, the owner of the complex, other tenants, children old enough to read, and an appropriate city official.

Be prepared to explain the differences among the six letters and your reasons for them in class, or to do so in an essay written in class.

C

College/Idea: Write an editorial of 50 to 75 words for your college newspaper explaining an idea you have that would improve the situation in your college in some way; gear your editorial to a *general audience.* Then rewrite it to suit your classmates, your professor(s), the dean, someone on the board of regents or other governing body of your school, and a suitable public official.

Be prepared to explain the differences among the six editorials and your reasons for them in class or to do so in an essay written in class.

D

Speech/Topic: Write a speech of 50 to 75 words explaining the idea of "love" to a *general audience*. Then rewrite the speech to give to an audience of boy scouts, of woman's libbers, of fraternity brothers, and of priests.

Be prepared to explain the differences among the speeches and your reasons for them in class, or to do so in an essay written in class.

EXERCISE 4

With the agreement of your instructor, select an author or poet for an intensive two-week study. For the first week read as much as you can of that person's work. Then, with the agreement of your instructor, select a reasonably short passage and try to analyze the writer's style: the kinds of sentences; the word choices; ths figures of speech, if any; the relationship to surrounding material; and so on.

Discuss your findings with your instructor and then write a 500- to 800-word theme about what you have learned.

It will be beneficial to you as you continue your study of writing in future courses to pay this kind of attention to the poets and playwrights and essayists and philosophers whose work you will study. What you learn about how others write and have written will help you as you strive to improve your own work.

a glossary of common writing problems and how to solve them

At one time or another, every writer (student or professional) finds it hard to get moving on a writing project. Sometimes you have a topic but cannot for the life of you think of a thing to say about it. Other times you have a topic and enough ideas, but you can't get organized enough to write the paragraphs. Other times, no matter what you do, you just can't get started at all.

No matter what your writing problem, there is usually a solution, and the solution is usually surprisingly easy to apply. You can use this glossary to help you diagnose specifically what your problem is and then select the appropriate course of action to deal with that problem. You will notice that the glossary is set up in checklist form to help you use it quickly and efficiently, and that most of the space is devoted to problems with rough-draft writing, since that is where you are most likely to get bogged down.

1. You Just Can't Get Started At All

Possible Reasons	What to Do
☐ *You misunderstood the assignment* (its complexity, length, due date, intent, relevance to other classwork, etc.).	1. Recheck notes on assignment. 2. Recheck relevant class notes. 3. Confer with a classmate. 4. Speak with your instructor. 5. Make sure you have not undertaken *more* than was assigned, thus making it harder for yourself (e.g., accidentally starting to analyze a whole essay rather than the assigned section).
☐ *You lack essential background* (relevant class lecture, relevant reading assignment not done, or important points overlooked).	1. Read or reread relevant assignments as appropriate; it is a good idea to at least skim reading assignments before attempting to write themes. 2. Get notes from a classmate or from instructor if necessary.
☐ *You don't understand the course in general* (textbooks too hard; lectures too difficult).	1. Catch up on any missed reading assignments (skim them to get main concepts and an idea of what you will have to learn). 2. Get class notes on missed lectures and discussion periods (sometimes your problem is that you were not there for an explanation of the basics). 3. Get an easier book for basic background (children's books and encyclopedias may help). 4. Investigate the possibility of tutoring from a professor or a classmate; some schools have tutorial services.
☐ *You know nothing about the topic* (no one can write about the unknown; interest is generated by specific knowledge).	1. Check textbooks, class notes, etc. 2. Speak with classmates, friends, instructor. 3. Use reference section of library for quick background (encyclopedias, children's books, other references).

Possible Reasons	*What to Do*
☐ *Personal problems may be in the way* (fear of failure or embarrassment; too tired to think; would rather be doing something else right now; feeling overwhelmed by the assignment; etc.).	1. Personal problems often must be resolved *before* you can concentrate on effective writing. 2. Writing is a skill that you *can* learn if you follow the procedures in this book; there is no reason to fear failure or embarrassment; mistakes are *not* the same as failure. 3. Plan your time, rescheduling or eliminating less valuable activities. 4. Make a reasonable writing time budget, allowing for sleep and other pursuits; it is often better to put your writing aside for awhile if you *really* don't feel like it and there is time. 5. Break the assignment down into small, manageable parts (e.g., "Today I will do the prewriting steps; tomorrow I will do . . .").
☐ *You're just plain stuck.*	1. You *can* get started if you will be patient and not lose your self-confidence. 2. Reassess the situation: Are you *sure* you understand the assignment? the readings? 3. Focus your attention on the prewriting steps: List ideas; limit your topic; try various thesis sentence approaches. 4. Review your class notes, assignments, research sources. 5. Take a break. Much writing is done in the subconscious. The idea you need might come to you if you relax for awhile. 6. Compare your topic with a random idea (e.g., "How is this assignment like a snake?"); it sounds silly, but if you genuinely list similarities and differences you may start your creative juices flowing. 7. Discuss the assignment with your instructor. You will find that most instructors are more than willing to help you, especially if you have made a determined effort to succeed on your own.

2. You Have a Topic but It Simply Won't Work

Possible Reasons	*What to Do*
☐ *You're trying to skip the prewriting steps.*	1. Prewriting steps help you accomplish your theme-writing work efficiently; they are not a waste of time. 2. Review the appropriate chapters in this book if need be. 3. Spend time listing ideas, working with your topic, and trying to develop your thesis sentence *before* attempting to "write" your theme.
☐ *You're not handling your topic properly.*	1. You want a limited, specific subcategory of an idea, one that has meaning and importance to you. 2. You need to express that topic idea in writing, clearly and precisely. 3. Review the appropriate chapters in this book if need be. 4. Don't try to skip the "writing it down" step, even if you think you can. Skipping steps will make writing harder for you.
☐ *You have selected an impossible topic.*	1. You have selected a topic that is too big or vague and have not limited it; limit the topic. 2. You have a monumental research project or one that is too hard or time-consuming; limit or abandon the topic.
☐ *You can't get interested in an assigned topic.*	1. Gather information (use books, magazines, notes, other people); knowledge generates interest. 2. Limit your topic; you may be expected to do that in any case. 3. Look for a new angle on your topic; a subtle change can make a big difference. 4. Spend some time working out a topic of similar difficulty and scope; then ask your instructor if you may use your own topic instead of the assigned one. 5. Develop your topic as if you were interested in it; you may wind up liking it after all.
☐ *You may be trying to start by writing an "introduction."*	1. Begin with your thesis sentence; if an introduction is needed, it should be written *after* the theme has been developed.

3. You Can't Develop Your Theme

Possible Reasons	*What to Do*
☐ *You can't write an effective thesis sentence.*	1. Limit and specify your topic. 2. Spend time listing ideas, especially predicate ideas. 3. It may help to alter your topic slightly so that you can make an assertion about it. 4. Reread the pertinent chapters in this book. 5. You may need to get further into the writing process for the final thesis sentence to develop; as long as your tentative thesis sentence is workable, use that to start with. 6. You may find it effective to begin by disagreeing with the opinion of an authority ("When G. B. Jones said that public transportation was not important, he was definitely wrong") or agreeing with a controversial opinion. You may get started by putting your thesis sentence into question form, or you may begin by trying to argue against your own point of view. Any of these methods may help you refine and express your ideas.
☐ *You can't structure your theme.*	1. Back up and repeat previous steps. Spend time thinking about your topic, listing ideas, limiting your topic, and redeveloping your thesis sentence. See if you can come up with a new twist to get you moving. 2. Reread the chapter about structuring your theme. Spend time developing topic sentences (try listing reasons why your thesis sentence is true—apply the "test of because"). If you can't develop topic sentences, you may need to spend some time gathering more information so that you will have something to say about your topic.

Possible Reasons	*What to Do*
☐ *You can't write your paragraphs.*	1. Reread the chapter about paragraphs. Remember that paragraphs can be built from details, facts, statistics, definitions, quotations, stories, anecdotes, reasons, explanations, and so on.
	2. Think of the *details* of why you believe that each topic sentence is true, and use those in your paragraphs.
	3. Spend time doing some thinking and research to gather the details you need.
☐ *Yes, but it still won't work.*	1. Don't try to be fancy; a rough draft does not have to be neat, though you must be able to read it yourself.
	2. Don't try to do it all in one sitting. Writing takes time, and time used in a certain way. You will get more benefit from an hour on Monday, an hour on Tuesday, and two hours on Wednesday than you would from a frantic "all-nighter." If it's already too late this time, do your best and let it go at that, but do make a writing budget for your next theme assignment.
	3. Remember that you are not planning to write "a rough draft" so much as "rough drafts." It is OK to tear something up and start again if you were heading in the wrong direction. Sometimes it's the only way.
☐ *You may be getting discouraged too soon.*	1. Take a break.
	2. You are not alone—everyone gets stuck from time to time.
	3. Maintain a confident attitude and keep trying.

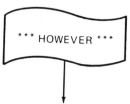

Possible Reasons	*What to Do*
	If you get more than halfway through the period that you have allotted to rough-draft writing and are still stumped in spite of your best efforts, *a conference with your instructor is in order*. Bring what you have done, and be prepared to explain your problem (sometimes writing problems are hard to verbalize). You will usually find that the solution appears within a few moments.

4. You Can't Revise Your Theme

Possible Reasons	*What to Do*
☐ *You need to learn what can be done to polish a theme.*	1. Read the second unit of this book.
☐ *You need to review some aspect of grammar.*	1. Ask your instructor to recommend a grammar textbook. Most grammatical problems can be eliminated with some work.
☐ *You have not allowed enough time for revision.*	1. Allow some time (preferably several days) between your acceptable rough draft and the revision process so that you may get a new perspective on what you've written. 2. Plan so that you will have enough writing time for a "rewrite" *and* for recopying your theme before submitting it. 3. If you can develop an acceptable rough draft, you *can* revise your theme if you allow enough time (and energy) to do so.

the main things to remember about writing college themes

☐ 1. The earlier you go wrong in the writing process, the further wrong you are likely to go, so don't skip the preliminary writing steps.

☐ 2. Get the assignment straight. You can cause yourself more unnecessary hassle by misunderstanding the assignment than in almost any other way.

☐ 3. Remember to budget your time so that you will have enough allotted to complete your assignment properly.

☐ 4. Spend the time necessary to develop a workable topic and an effective thesis sentence.

☐ 5. Use the "test of because" to help you develop topic sentences.

☐ 6. Use subdivision and charting to generate, evaluate, and control your ideas.

☐ 7. Relax as you write your rough drafts; it will help.

☐ 8. Leave some time between the rough drafts and the revision process.

☐ 9. Proofreading your finished, neatly typed theme will help you make a good impression with your work.

☐ 10. Your greatest asset as a writer is your self-confidence; if you follow the procedures you have learned in this book, you *can* write an effective college theme.

80 81 82 9 8 7 6 5 4 3 2 1